A Child Laughs

With much
love, and
thanks for
years of friendship!
Richard

A Child Laughs

PRAYERS
OF JUSTICE
AND HOPE

Maria Mankin and Maren C. Tirabassi

THE PILGRIM PRESS
CLEVELAND

The Pilgrim Press, 700 Prospect Avenue, Cleveland, Ohio 44115
thepilgrimpress.com
© 2017 by Maria Mankin and Maren C. Tirabassi

Printed in the United States of America on acid-free paper

19   18   17   16   15   5   4   3   2   1

ISBN 978-0-8298-2032-4

CONTENTS

A Child's Laugh

My grandson giggles—
and it's some funny song of mine,
a tickled foot,
a smile mirror to my smile,
the dog's silliness,
the infinitely repeatable humor
of something falling on the floor,
or just the way sunlight
tinkerbelles on leaf
or the shiny car seat buckle.

And I think,
this is what Mary hoped
when she belted
magnificat in second soprano—
not just her precious
and most intimate joy—
one baby, one face smiling down,
but a wild hope,

a wild, almost unimaginable,
a wild and ordinary hope
of a heart
turned inside out—

that whenever one child is laughing,
there be the possibility
for the happy laughter
of every child in the world.

How can we shape a world so that every child will have a reason to laugh?

Isaiah's holy mountain prophecy in Isaiah 11 that names reconciliation between all of God's children and even within the natural world culminates with the image of a toddler playing above a rattlesnake's hole. Mary's song is not so much a lucky-me pregnancy song as it is her recognition, as soon as she carries a child, that justice should extend to all the hungry and the poor. A strange story in 1 Kings 3, often cited as proof of Solomon's wisdom, actually describes a true parent as one who will never find acceptable the death of any child. Jesus agrees, naming his family as the ones who do God's will, insisting his followers put a child in their midst, and even accepting the miraculous generosity of one child's lunch.

This—the longing not just for survival, but for laughter—is at the center of *A Child Laughs—Prayers of Justice and Hope.*

This book of fifty-two reflections was gathered in a community process. Some eighty people offered more than a hundred suggestions of themes or issues or concerns they felt were crucial to hope and justice for all people in all places. Some are very specific: Psalm 78 for Zimbabwe; the legacy of Indian Residential Schools in Canada; gun violence and police militarization in the United States; healing from childhood sexual abuse; compassionate care for species extinction; street ministry. Other themes—like cultural diversity, or living in an overstressed world, faithful anger, or standing up for an all-inclusive God—are more expansive.

We then offered an open invitation to writers to address these themes, and seventy-seven responded. Some overlapped the group that crowd-sourced the issues, though many were new. These writers came from eleven different countries, and many wrote collegially with a partner they had only met electronically. The brief biographical words at the end of each reflection are not footnotes, but a celebration of the possibility of enthusiastic and wonderful community. The writers prayed their way into each subject from personal perspectives, some focusing on a future for all ages, all traditions, all communities, others focusing on issues of childhood or addressing the Christian faith community particularly. Each offering is loosely similar and radically unique. It's no surprise that the most common and independently chosen text was Psalm 139: "you have searched me and known me . . . I am fearfully and wonderfully made."

Fifty-one of these reflections are shaped with a background statement, a personal prayer, a faith community resource, which is often liturgy, and questions for reflection and action. The final chapter is a gathering of single prayers about issues that weren't chosen for more expansive discussion in the book. *A Child Laughs* can be read privately week by week through the year, or as a book to share in a small group during Lent or the summer. It not only challenges thoughts and prayers but also invites action and, we hope, a change of heart.

We are grateful to the original contributors of ideas, the remarkable writers who put up with our herding their wild creativity into some useful conformity, the gifted and supportive folks at The Pilgrim Press who believed in this project, Kris Firth and Rick Porter for their remarkable creative gifts on this volume, our own families who shared their time with this strange global collaborative, and the ever brooding and birthing presence of the Holy Spirit who reminded us again and again not just to pray and work for hope and justice, but also to laugh.

I ✳ FAITHFUL ANGER

I no longer believe in an angry God;
that would make you too much in my image.
Rather, you are the God who can hear my cussing tongue broken and choked
And I have no fear that I will offend you.

Many of us learned that we are not to be angry, that this strong emotion frightens others and is not "nice." We've been taught that anger is a sin, and we fracture God's Shalom (Realm) if we voice our anger. Love is the greatest commandment, and we often consider anger the opposite of love. Yet anger, used faithfully, can be a form of love: love of God, love of others, love of self. Prophets and psalmists used anger to express necessary truths—why can't we?

When we grow angry, we realize our boundaries have been violated. Sometimes another person has crossed our boundaries; sometimes a society's behaviors impinge on our holy selves; sometimes we violate our own values. If we stop to listen to it, we might learn that anger comes from fear (a child who has run into the street) or pain (a friend who has misinterpreted or dismissed our intentions) or injustice (culturally established discriminations). A sense of powerlessness often provokes us.

Anger is not hatred. Yet our responses to anger can sometimes come out as hateful. Loving forms of anger cannot be turned against God, neighbor, or self. Faithful anger is not the out-of-control feeling that seeks to annihilate all in its path. Holy anger can teach us and grow us and can be a tool for building the Shalom of God in this world.

not thunder and lightning
not the slow burn of coals in my belly
not a rushing tsunami of emotion
anger blows stronger
burns deeper
rushes wilder than these

anger unfurls like the slow petals of my peony—
packed tighter than onion skin and as acrid

and then it blooms

I live in the United States, but there are parallel situations everywhere. In my context we've been acknowledging anger in communities that are tired of living under unjust status quo. People of color cannot quietly accept the day-to-day slights, unequal systems, and outright prejudice that our nation perpetuates. Gender minorities are claiming full humanity and an expectation to be seen and named as God's beloved. Hard-working citizens express desire for security. Sometimes our anger emerges in raised voices, protest gatherings. Anger should be listened to and recognized as a person claiming their limits.

PERSONAL PRAYER

Let me rage, Mighty Spirit. Let me shout and tremble and stomp in a tantrum of my own powerlessness. Let me spew the atrocity of insults I've absorbed from within me. Let my fury be catharsis.

And then let me feel. Let me taste the burning tears of hurt and healing. Let me understand—not just me, but him or her or them or you. Let me empathize with where this force comes from. Let me recognize it as love.

And then let me heal. Let me heal this inner fuse. Let me heal the outer brokenness. Let me heal the connection that intertwines you, me, all . . .

COMMUNITY PRAYER

A Litany of Confession and Hope

ONE: We are angry.

ALL: Angry at you, God.

ONE: Angry that you are not a deity who stretches a mighty fist to smite.

ALL: We've claimed your anger for generations,
calling it righteousness—

ONE: but it is not you; it is we who are angry.

ALL: So fuel our anger for what is right!

ONE: Right relationship with the earth:

ALL: We rage against coal ports and pipelines;
meanwhile, we pesticide our produce.

ONE: Right relationship between nations:

ALL: We rage at war brutality;
then we strike politicians with vicious tongues.

ONE: Right relationship among ethnicities:

ALL: We rage for black lives to matter;
and those who are white deny the privileges of race.

ONE: Right relationship between religions:

ALL: We rage for Muslim equality;
yet we deride our own faith siblings.

ONE: Right relationship for sex and gender:

ALL: We rage against GLBTQ atrocities;
meanwhile, we diminish powerful advocates for change.

ONE: We feel anger at others so quickly, Holy One,
and we forget to turn that righteous rage on our own actions.

ALL: We perpetuate pain without realizing, even as we work for justice.
Love us anyway, God. And, through your love, heal us.
Heal our forgetfulness, even as we remember to use our anger justly.

Assurance of Grace
ONE: God's power envelopes our whole beings—even our righteous rage. Spirit's love embraces our wounds and moves us forward toward the Christ's Beloved Community.
ALL: **Be at peace, one and all. We are forgiven.**

Prayer for Illumination
God of the psalmist and prophet, invite us into your understanding of when to speak loving truth with anger. The welcome mat is muddy with those who have entered before us. Through the open door of listening—despite our fears—we will sit at table with your justice. Amen

⤕ • ⤔

QUESTIONS FOR REFLECTION/ACTION

1. What does anger feel like for you, and where is it in your body? Is it a burn or a stone in your gut, your chest? A tingle on your skin? Have you deeply listened to it telling you its reason for being? Can you offer your anger gratitude for speaking where your boundaries have been crossed?

2. When have you allowed your anger to become hateful? What forgiveness must you seek? How could you attempt reconciliation or make reparation?

3. How might the Spirit use your anger to bring God's Shalom more clearly into being? Where will you use your anger with loving care for your community? For yourself?

⤕ • ⤔

Sharon A. Benton lives and plays in the most beautiful place she could ever dream of, surrounded by waves and mountains and fuzzy-mossed giant trees. She serves as lead pastor among phenomenal colleagues and members at First Congregational Church of Bellingham, Washington.

2 ✸ CLAIMING WHOLENESS IN A BROKEN AND VIOLENT WORLD

Some of God's children read about violence from a distance, while others experience its devastation firsthand, on a daily basis. Although the Bible includes stories of God-sanctioned violence, Christians do well to look to the threads of healing, peacemaking, reconciliation, and grace that are woven together so beautifully by and in Jesus of Nazareth.

In the Hebrew prophets, in the Psalms, in Christ and those who gave their lives to following him, we find ancient-yet-new visions of peace and wholeness, both within the individual and throughout God's world, that can sustain and lift us up when violence wears us down.

PERSONAL PRAYER

God of holy wholeness,
I long for your healing.
For myself, my family,
my community and nation,
my people and so many others,
this world of brokenness and pain.
I see so much violence and suffering,
as unhealed wounds
fester into hostility,
anger clung to for vindication
snarls and hardens into bitterness,

fear and pride and greed and envy
compete for first place
among the idols of our hearts,
warning us of scarcity,
triggering survival instincts,
drawing lines and boundaries
that must not be crossed
or else.
I see this sickness
no less in myself than in my enemies.
Retribution, arrogance, cynicism, prejudice,
shame, victimhood, apathy, despair . . .
The world has battered and beaten me,
taken those I treasured, taught me to hate,
taught me to become hard and small
and self-contained.
Yet when I turn to you,
you do not shout
to compete with these voices.
You do not throw your force around
to overwhelm the unconvinced.
You make the sun to shine and the rain to fall
on the just and unjust alike.
And I do not understand.
This is not the justice I long for.
But the longer I look to you,
listen for you, sit with you,
the more I hear your still small voice
whisper,
Peace.
Take heart.
In this world you will know suffering.
But have courage.
I have overcome the world.
You are my own beloved child,

precious in my sight.
Before you were born, I knew you.
When you were being knit together
in your mother's womb,
I loved you and called you by name.
You are fearfully and wonderfully made,
bearing my divine image,
love made flesh once more.
Beneath your brokenness,
you are still whole.
Beyond your hopelessness,
you have strength to rise again.
Beside your loneliness,
I will companion you,
walking with you, giving you strength,
singing the song of your soul,
so that you may carry on
with the work, and the gifts
that are yours
to do, to give, to bless the world.
Take courage, my child.
You are not alone.
And I still do not understand.
But it is enough,
and I am thankful.
Amen.

COMMUNITY PRAYER

Holy, Whole, and Healing God,
You are our source and our end.
You have created and claimed us,
called us your beloved children.
We praise you for your steadfast love,
and your vision of wholeness
for all people and all of creation.

Yet we struggle to maintain our faith,
our sense of trust and peace and worthiness
in light of the violence that wracks our world.
Some among us today are wounded and hurting,
from physical, spiritual, or emotional violence,
while others are struggling with brokenness
experienced in different ways.
Help us now to see ourselves as you see us,
to center ourselves in your grace,
that we might know how deeply you care for us
and be restored to a sense of our own wholeness
and renewed by your steadfast love.

God of Holy Wholeness and Healing,
our hearts ache for the world around us.
In our families, our community,
our nation and other nations,
violence takes a daily toll,
as we fail to see your image in one another,
or reinforce dividing lines between our sisters and brothers.
We lift up in prayer to you now
those people and places
we know to be in particular need of your healing presence . . .

Healing, Whole, and Holy God,
you offer healing that we don't always understand,
to reach the deep and broken places
in ourselves and in the world.
You call us to find wholeness
not only for ourselves
but for all of creation
in the practice of compassion, justice,
peace, and reconciliation.
In Jesus Christ you have shown us what it means
to embrace a holiness that is inclusive, not exclusive;
to break down dividing walls

and replace them with bridges of understanding.
May we see our lives and our world
as whole, and holy,
interdependent and mutually connected.
May we become channels of your healing peace
through which you proclaim
 of your love
and your desire for fullness of life
that we have known in Jesus Christ.
We pray in his name, our Prince of Peace,
Redeemer, Reconciler, and One who binds us into the family of God.
Amen

→> • <←

QUESTIONS FOR REFLECTION/ACTION

1. What words or practices help you connect with a deep sense
   of inner peace or wholeness? How might you weave these into
   the regular rhythms of your life?

2. What kinds of violence most affect your particular community?
   What are the differences between being a member of a group that
   has experienced violence or brokenness and being an ally or
   companion to such a community? Given these differences, how
   might you pray or take action to resist violence with love?

3. When might claiming wholeness look more like disruption or
   conflict than traditional images of peace? What role does anger
   have to play in the work for wholeness and healing?

→> • <←

Kerry L. Greenhill is an ordained deacon in the United Methodist Church who seeks
to illuminate the holy wholeness of life. She loves reading, television costume dramas,
tea, and dark chocolate and lives with her family and two cats in Colorado.

3 THE POLITICAL IS PERSONAL

In the 1960s and '70s, many women in many nations were challenging individual understandings and social structures that had worked, and continued to work, to make them second-class citizens. Feminist thought recognized that inequalities of gender, of sex, of sexuality, of race, of class, of ability—of these and more—were interconnected. Each woman's history, each woman's personal life experience and experience of oppression, was key to understanding systems and patterns of oppression. Out of this understanding came the words "the personal is political." I wonder sometimes if the opposite isn't also true—the political is personal.

In the broadest sense, politics are the structures and rules that groups of people agree to use to live together. In this sense, families are political bodies, book clubs are political bodies, nations are political bodies—churches are political bodies, too. (Anyone who has ever been part of a congregation's decision-making body has experienced the joy and pain of this!)

As people of Jesus' Way, each part of our personal story is deeply entwined in Jesus' story. We have the wonderful, and sometimes difficult, task of living God's love with every moment of our lives. What might that mean for our politics—not just the politics between nations, or in nations, but the politics of our towns, our communities, and our relationships?

PERSONAL PRAYER

This moment
is a momentous moment,
God.
I'm standing here,
ready to make my mark.
A lever pulled, an X made, a fingerprint smudged,
a hand raised,
or an "aye" to be voiced . . .
this is a moment that will change the world.
A momentous moment.
Will I buy that shirt, made by the labour of children;
will I raise my voice to challenge the unchallengeable;
will I laugh *with* an elder,
or offer my strength to lift someone up—
this is a moment that will change the world.
A momentous moment.
Can I be the song that sings out hope?
Can I be the life that lives in love?
Can I be one who is part of the many
who truly care about the Other,
and celebrate them for who they truly are—
this is a moment that will change the world.
A momentous moment.
Be with me, God.
I pray.

COMMUNITY PRAYER
Call to Worship

ONE: *Ora et labora.* Prayer and work.
They go hand in hand—
in this place and in the world.

ALL: Let us raise our hands in worship and work.
Let us raise our voices and celebrate God.

ONE: The personal is political.
My story, your story, Christ's story.
Living and alive—
in this place and in the world.

ALL: **Let us raise our hearts in worship and work.
Let us raise our voices and celebrate God.**

ONE: The political is personal.
Each of us one voice,
together a great choir—
loving God, and loving the other,
as we love ourselves.

ALL: **Let us raise our spirits in worship and work.
Let us raise our voices and celebrate God!**

ONE: Alleluia!
ALL: **Alleluia! Amen!**

Blessing and Sending Forth (Benediction and Commissioning)
ONE: Creator says, "Children! Go where I send you."

ALL: **How will you send *me*?**

ONE: I'm going to send you, one by one,

ALL: **to the lines and the booths,
where decisions are spun,**

ONE: all for the little bitty babies—born, born . . .

ALL: **born throughout the land.**

ONE: Christ says, "Disciples! Go where I send you."

ALL: **How will you send me?**

ONE: I'm going to send you, two or more,

ALL: **to live my love, step through that door,
in challenge, in joy, with voices that roar—**

ONE: all for the little bitty babies—born, born . . .

ALL: born throughout the land.

One: Holy Spirit says, "People! Go where I send you!"

ALL: How will you send us?

ONE: I'm going to send you, but never alone,
to new places dance (or even be blown!)—

ALL: all for the little bitty babies—
born, born, born
throughout the land!

⇥ ● ⇤

QUESTIONS FOR REFLECTION/ACTION

1. Some of us live in countries that celebrate many cultures and recognize many faiths lived by their citizens. How do we support people living out their faith in the public, political sphere?

2. What is one action that you could take, to help your community to make just, equitable, loving decisions?

3. Who are the people whose stories you need to hear, in your family, your church, your community, or your country? How could you go about listening to them? How could you go about being an ally for change?

⇥ ● ⇤

A pastor, poet, and liturgical writer, **Richard Bott** serves in ministry with the United Church of Canada in Vancouver, British Columbia. He celebrates that people find his words helpful in their ministries.

4 ✳ FULL INCLUSION OF THOSE WITH INTELLECTUAL AND DEVELOPMENTAL DISABILITIES

The justice challenge is right there in the word: disabled. It's a label that names others for what they cannot do. How many of us would like to be known in that way? I might be "the guy who isn't athletic" or "the one who can't speak Spanish." Instead, the spiritual community invites us to experience each other through our gifts, including our gifts of brokenness and need.

Our congregation has a group for adults with intellectual and developmental disabilities. They bring tremendous gifts to the community. They plant flowers in our courtyard, send bookmarks to people who are sick, and play chimes in worship. They also give us the gift of caring for them and the gift of reminding us that we can also ask for help. When people who have been called disabled are included as members of the church with something to contribute, all of us become better able to claim our giftedness and our vulnerability.

PERSONAL PRAYER

I have learned to see holes; practiced looking for deficiencies; gotten good at asking, "What is wrong with this picture?" Wherever I turn my eyes, something appears to be missing. My wife has forgotten to buy milk. My daughter still isn't crawling. My friend refuses to pick me up at the airport. I see selfishness, incompetence, disability.

Looking at myself, I am also full of holes. I am distracted by my cell phone. I haven't jogged in months. I have forgotten to buy milk. I am selfish, incompetent, unable.

The holes I see begin to block out everything else. They become the whole. And I become convinced that the world is ugly, mean, and small.

But that cannot be. Because you are its creator and completer, and everyone I see is made in your image. Refocus my eyes. Teach me to see what is, rather than what is not; to ask what is right and to give thanks for what is right here. Inspire in me a sense of gratitude for all that surrounds the holes.

For my wife, my daughter, my friend, myself, I give thanks. For all people and all creation, whom you have already declared good, I give thanks. For you, who are loving us to completeness, I give thanks.

COMMUNITY PRAYER

Doxology for my Friends with Intellectual and Developmental Disabilities

Praise God for your surprise hugs
    and your spontaneous dancing!
Praise God for your ready tears
    and your deep feeling!
Praise God for your fierce competitiveness
    and your stubborn loyalty!
Praise God for your earnest enthusiasm
    and your shameless vulnerability!
For your acceptance of help and your rejection of cynicism,
    your unqualified self-confidence and un-ironic joy,
For the way in which seeing your gifts rightly
    teaches me to look at myself and this beautiful world differently,
Praise God! Praise God! Praise God!

A Few Intercessions for Us All *by Maren Tirabassi*

For playgrounds where a person with an older body and a younger spirit can enjoy a good time without parents pulling their younger kids away, teaching everyone that it is all right for even play to be intolerant—

God of the see-saw of joy and pain, hear our prayer.

For employers willing to give a simple job to someone who will love it, stay with it, smile in it, and look a little different to the public—

God, sweeper of the lost, who knows how precious a coin is, hear our prayer.

For day programs with creativity, sheltered housing with beautiful views, Special Olympics and special "artistics," volunteer opportunities eager to welcome dog walkers, shelf stackers, bracelet makers, coffee pourers, trail markers—

God, who said "like a child" was the center, and everything else just perimeter, hear our prayer.

For protection from bullying, shaming, and belittling, for protection from financial, sexual, legal, and physical abuse, and for all the care that must come afterwards when those things happen—

God of the cross and resurrection, hear our prayer.

For police who understand the autism spectrum, for companions who learn to keep themselves safe, for aging parents who worry about the future, and for churches who hear the words . . . Down syndrome, cerebral palsy, fetal alcohol spectrum, pervasive developmental disorder, intellectual disability just like . . . born in Iowa, gluten intolerant, loves Mozart and lasagna, had a tough religious background, tender after a divorce, wins at fantasy football—keys to shape a personalized welcome and open the door—

God of the come-unto-me, hear our prayer. Amen.

➤ • ◄

QUESTIONS FOR REFLECTION/ACTION

1. What gifts have you received this week from the people around you?

2. Where in your life have you been focused on disability rather than on giftedness, on what is missing rather than what is present? How might it transform your relationship to another or to yourself to change that focus?

3. In what way are brokenness and need gifts that we can offer to one another?

→⇥ ● ⇤←

Vince Amlin is a minister at Bethany UCC in Chicago and church planter at Gilead Church Chicago, a community that worships beautifully, shares good food, and tells true stories that save lives (www.gileadchicago.org). He is grateful to his brother, Curtis Metzger, for all the lessons on (dis)ability.

Maren C. Tirabassi is a writer of liturgy, poetry, and fiction whose passion is anthology —putting the words and stories of others together. A United Church of Christ clergyperson, she is also a workshop facilitator and writing coach.

IN THE IMAGE OF GOD
GOD'S PEOPLE WITH MENTAL ILLNESS

5

Our sisters and brothers who experience mental illness are frequently stigmatized and may suffer from concomitant unemployment, homelessness, addictions, and broken relationships. Though we all experience brokenness, it can seem as if some kinds of brokenness are more "acceptable" in the public eye than others. From PTSD to depression, bipolar disorder to schizophrenia, multiple personality disorder to phobias and anxiety, we often fear what we do not or cannot understand.

Scriptural interpretation has sometimes portrayed the mentally ill as having "hidden sin." And yet, while the causes of mental anguish and suffering are legion, the truly demonic force is the lack of adequate treatment and resources for those of us with mental illness to both improve well-being and improve education around mental health issues.

Ostracism, disregard, misunderstanding, and inadequate treatment and care can all contribute to often tragic outcomes for those diagnosed with mental illness. It does not need to remain so. Indeed, befriending those who suffer from mental illness is a powerful first step that can bring encouragement and hope, even when the illness is protracted, complicated, or compounded by addiction or other pain-filled issues.

PERSONAL PRAYER

Rebirth

She lies awake on the gurney.
"Drink this," the emergency room nurse kindly says.
Black charcoal in a Styrofoam cup, thick with water,
a tonic for toxic overdose.
"Would you like some soda to wash it down?"
The girl weakly shakes her head, pauses—
then sips carefully, as if it were nectar
worth savoring.
A good sign, they say.
She does not resist,
another sign.
Her mind wanders,
This is my body
"My body," the girl declares to no one in particular,
but the nurse hears,
turns and smiles.
Another sign if you choose to view it that way.
For every completed suicide there are these,
countless others, found and unfound,
who perceive their attempts at self-destruction
or even preservation—
as another failed solution, and despair.
It would be months, possibly years,
before the girl returned to herself.
No longer beaten down by a loss of control
over ruthless voices twisting daggers inside
Yet it began *then*—
with that charcoal and that nurse,
the one who, despite a long shift and far too many patients,
a difficult spouse, and paltry paycheck,
bends now tenderly over blackened, trembling lips
which remain mute

as she gently wipes away the stain and whispers,
"I, too, was desperate once."

Suggested Reading: Romans 12:2

Oh God, guard my speech that I may choose carefully the words I use.
Let me refrain from calling *anyone*
bonkers, nutcase, batshit crazy, demented, crazed,
maniac, twisted, mental, or raving mad.
Let me avoid hurling epithets like "she's got a loose screw"
or idioms that say "he is off his rocker."
Keep me from twirling my finger at the end of my ear like a twirling
    ribbon
Chide me from forgetting that each are made in your image
and what is light to me may not be so very light to another,
For every descriptive that points to someone losing her mind,
could I instead use words that affirm our shared humanity,
that demonstrate compassionate regard,
and respect our genuine difference and diversity?
Or could I simply say nothing at all?
Could you help me with this one thing, God?
Remind me that we are all beautifully broken,
and that those with mental illness
are some of the bravest fighters
I could ever hope to know.
Guard my speech, Holy One.
Give me a mind that is on the mend.

COMMUNITY PRAYER

Suggested Reading: Luke 4:41

Litany of Intercession
ONE: For the one who disassociates, suffers a fragmented identity
as a finely-honed defense against untold harm—

MANY: Jesus casts out the demons of abuse and neglect,
brings care and community close at hand.

ONE: For the one who, even now, questions his own worth or her beloved status
in a world that ties worth to salary
and human dignity to near constant productivity,

MANY: **Jesus casts out the demons of societal expectation and accumulation,
brings care and community close at hand.**

ONE: For the one who cannot remember to take one tiny pill a day,
but who rages at memories too difficult to forget,
railing at the family dysfunction that was not her fault,

MANY: **Jesus casts out the demons of memory and molestation,
brings care and community close at hand.**

ONE: For the grief-stricken and angry, for the manic and obsessed,
for the body dysmorphic or detached, coded and coping,

MANY: **Jesus casts out the demons that label but fail to love,
and brings care and community close at hand.**

ONE: For the mental anguish we admit
and the unwanted thoughts that we fear to name,

MANY: **Jesus casts out all demons that diminish God's people,
bringing care and community close at hand.**

Suggested Reading: Mark 3:21, Luke 8:2b

Confession

Holy Jesus, you knew how closely individual well-being is tied to communal well-being. Today we confess to you how we have compounded the difficulty of mental illness. We have broken the bruised reed and placed more grievous burdens on the downhearted.

We confess now the demon of fear that possesses us—fear that too often incarcerates the mentally ill rather than medically treating their sickness.

We confess now the demon of judgment, choosing to believe that those who are mentally ill are not deserving of our time or resources, or even our friendship.

We confess now the demon of racism, forgetting that when dreams are allowed to die, the human spirit can wither and lash out from the blow.

We confess now the demon of bigotry that treats mental illness in the other—other by race or religion or gender identity—as more to be blamed than the mental illness in those like ourselves.

We confess now the demon of self-importance, priding ourselves with our things and excuses, rather than undertaking action to lessen the sorrows of existence and increasing the beauty of human welfare.

We confess now the demon of stinginess, clinging and hoarding resources that could help to free our struggling sisters and brothers.

We confess now the demon of ostracism, choosing to stigmatize, isolate, and unfriend, rather than befriending and drawing close.

We confess now our violence, choosing to send our loved ones and young into harm's way, without adequately funding the healing of their moral injuries and suffering spirit upon return.

Lord Jesus, you were once believed to be out of your mind . . . and yet, you knew sanity also depended on a healthy community of belonging and met need. Carry us, from our spiritual wounds to mutual healing, that all may be reconciled within your holy mind and that all may be transformed within your divine heart.

Amen

Assurance of Grace

As one identified with healing from seven demons became the first witness to the resurrection, so may our changes of heart help us acknowledge the Easter in each other's lives.

→ • ←

QUESTIONS FOR REFLECTION/ACTION

1. What is your experience with mental illness?

2. If you are a pastor, lay worship leader or Bible study facilitator or participant, how would you carefully approach passages in scripture like the Gerasene demoniac (Mark 5:1–17 and Luke 8:26–37), knowing that sisters and brothers in your faith community may be intimately struggling with mental illness and its effects? How do you parse the frequent biblical relationship between sin and suffering, demon possession and the mentally ill?

3. How do you understand mental illness as an illness both like other illnesses and also different from other illnesses?

4. How can you address suicide without criminalizing it (that is, saying one committed suicide*) and without lessening its impact on survivors?

The National Association for Mental Illness (NAMI) suggests "died by suicide" to journalists.

⤛ • ⤜

Dee Ledger is a pastor serving Bethesda (Maryland) United Church of Christ. A single mother of young twin boys, she enjoys writing, collage, coloring, quiet Sabbath time, and those impromptu paint classes that promise that "You, too, can paint!" She survived the loss of a son and husband through the kindness of strangers and friends and is intimately familiar with the incredible beauty that shines through losses of all kinds.

6 ✳ COMPASSIONATE CARE FOR THOSE WHO ARE CHRONICALLY ILL

It's hard enough to have a discrete health need, a broken bone, or a passing illness that invades our bodies and takes us from our daily rhythms, requiring time, attention, resources and care. How much more difficult it is when a long-term and progressive illness settles in, causing life to change in both large and small ways.

This is hard enough. But while some people have a support team with time and willingness to help, others find themselves desperate and isolated, without access to good care. Some may have the resources to purchase what is needed, but many others struggle to get medicine, equipment, and even caregivers.

Suggested Reading: Psalm 139:7–14a

PERSONAL PRAYER

God, it is hard
when sickness extends beyond the acute
and makes itself at home in the bodies that are home to us.

We settle into unsought rhythms,
life seemingly reduced to messy necessities
and we feel so alone.

God, it is hard
when small comforts and mundane tasks
require resources that we do not have.

It is hard
when the value of our lives
seems measured by what help
    what time
    what comfort
we can afford to hire.

We know that we are your beloved children,
that your love for us is not measured by our wealth or our family
or our connections.

We know that you are with us
at the farthest limits of possibility
in heaven, in sheol, in all the in-between places

in bed and bathroom and wheelchair
in closed-in spaces of illness and caregiving
even in the valley of the shadow of death
but we yearn for health in body, mind, and spirit.
We yearn for breath and laughter and sunshine and freedom.
Help us to reach for what is needed.
Help us to claim for ourselves
    love
    joy
    goodness
    health.

Remind us that you are in both storm and stillness
speaking peace, speaking comfort, speaking hope.
Remind us that you love us beyond reason.
Remind us that you love us beyond death.
Amen

COMMUNITY PRAYER

Prayer of Confession

God, we confess that we do not like to be confronted with things we
cannot fix.
We are tempted to speak platitudes, pretending that you never give
anyone more than they can handle.
We like easy solutions tied up with neat bows
    and it is hard for us to sit with someone who will not be healed.

We confess that we have time and talents we have hoarded for ourselves.
We confess that we are embarrassed by messy eating;
    we are embarrassed by smells and by forgetfulness.

We confess that out of sight too often really is out of mind.
We confess that we would rather recommend services
        in our mistaken certainty—
that there must be enough
that someone else must supply time, resources, and care
that our social net cannot possibly have such large holes
that the desperation we see is only for lack of knowledge
that we ourselves cannot possibly fill the gap

We confess that we would rather do some practical thing and be done.
because it is easier to bring a casserole, send some flowers,
or write a card
than it is to engage in messy relationships for the long haul.

Forgive us when we prescribe for ourselves
ways to think about the situations of others
rather than sharing them in full complexity. Amen

Assurance of Grace

God comes to us again and again, clearing our understanding, like a log
in the eye, so that we can respond to the many splinters of complication
in chronic and acute health situations of those around us.

Prayer of Intercession

Mother God, Father God, Creator and Sustainer,
We entrust to your care all those who sorrow or suffer.
>   those who are facing crises which threaten to overwhelm them,
>   those who are lonely or hurting, those who are in need.
Fill them with the joy of your presence;
>   Use us as your arms and your hands to minister to them.
We ask that you forgive us and heal us
>   fill us and transform us
So that we might love and serve all of your beloved children
>   and praise you not only with our lips
>   but with our very lives.
Amen

→➤ • ◄←

QUESTIONS FOR REFLECTION/ACTION

1. Do you remember a time in your life when you were desperate: when there weren't enough resources to go around, when you felt isolated or overwhelmed? What, if anything, did friends or neighbours do that was helpful for you? What did you not find helpful? What do you wish they had offered?

2. Who in your community has been struggling with chronic illness, either their own or that of a loved one—a child or an adult? Besides health, what might they be yearning for? a hot meal? easy company? the ability to get out and get away? inclusion? listening?

3. What discrete thing can you offer them without it being a way to "check the situation off your list"? What ongoing (or weekly or monthly) action might you offer?

→➤ • ◄←

Jamie L. Spriggs entered ministry as her third and final calling, after pursuing careers in French and in academic technology. She currently lives on a pretty lake with her dog, where she enjoys canoeing, hiking, and taking photos of beautiful sunsets.

VISITING THE GARDEN
ADDRESSING ADDICTION

I n the entire realm of human activity—profession and family situation, economic stability, spiritual foundation and academic achievement, race, gender, age, sexual orientation—one thing remains true. Alcoholism and substance addiction do not discriminate. Across many boundaries it doles out a broad spectrum of suffering. Many people experience their addictions compounded by guilt and stigma and the burden of "less than"—less than a capable loving child, less than a selfless partner, less than a hard-working person of dignity, less than an attentive parent.

In the halls of twelve-step programs such as Alcoholics Anonymous and Narcotics Anonymous, parents in recovery sit and listen to experience, strength, and hope, and work to change thoughts and behaviors that may have contributed to their addiction. Children sit with quiet toys, color, or do homework. Babies sleep in strollers, and toddlers play in portable playpens. Snacks in small plastic containers sit beside the ever-present disposable cup half-filled with coffee. Working to stay clean and sober one day at a time has become a life-saving new normal for parent and child alike.

PERSONAL PRAYER

On the way home from an AA meeting, a girl, never looking up from the doll in her lap, asked her mother a question. She said, "That man who stood up and talked to everyone, he said he used to be a garden variety drunk. What does that mean?"

Her mother, newly sober and attending a meeting every day, answered, "Garden variety means 'nothing special' or 'the same as everyone else.' It means 'ordinary' or 'regular.'"

Her daughter thought this over. Finally, she replied. "It doesn't make sense. A garden isn't full of things that are all the same. A garden is full of beautiful special wonderful things. Even our tomato plants are different from each other. One is tall and the other is short. One has big tomatoes and the other has little cherry tomatoes."

Her mother tried to explain. "I see what you mean, but a real garden is full of plants. Garden variety means all the same, like all plants are the same. Even different kinds of plants are still plants."

"Momma, you should look carefully at the plants in gardens. In our garden all the plants are different. And besides, there's more than just plants there. What about the anthills? There's big and small beetles, and red and brown worms. There's this spider that makes the most amazing webs, and in the morning the web looks like it has diamonds in it. One of the herb plants smells like a mint cookie when the wind blows. There's about ten different colors of green in the leaves and stems and buds. Plus really tiny rocks in white and grey and even blue!"

Her mother thought about the people in the halls of AA. There are old and young, highly educated and high-school dropouts, white, black, Latino, Chinese. Professionals and the unemployed sit together and share reflections. Able-bodied help the ailment-laden. Some are sick and tired and some are enthusiastic and grateful. Alcoholism found them all and no two were alike.

They all came to recovery on different paths too. Some traveled through dark and damp, like the rich topsoil that houses the seed. Some walked through hard and sharp stones dug from patches of promise. Some sat reflecting a breezy sense of relief and others the lush greens of newly mown attitudes. Some entered the doors covered in stubborn thorns, and then there were those with open petals of hope.

"Really, Momma, the only thing that's the same in our garden is that it's always you and me that take care of everything that lives there."

"You're right. Maybe that's what 'garden variety' means. Maybe it means we're all similar because we all depend on a Gardener who takes care of every plant, each one special and beautiful in its own way."

A PRAYER FOR CLERGY WITH PROCESSING ADDICTIONS *by Stephen G. Price*

O Comforting Healing God,

So many of us came to You first in our childhood, out of our deep pain. Neglected or abandoned, abused physically or sexually: we found safety, love, and sanctuary among the people of God. We felt Your love and Your tenderness surrounding us in the warmth and love of VBS, Sunday school, and youth leaders. We felt loved and at home, and we determined to follow and serve You. We became pastors, Christian educators, youth directors, and missionaries.

But we found that the ways we had learned to soothe ourselves against all that pain followed us into our adult lives—sex, food, gambling, compulsive shopping, Internet, self-harm—a multitude of secret driven behaviors that we tucked away in small pockets of our being hoping that they would never be seen. But they haunt and shame us.

Some of us have found help in recovery groups and therapy but some of us still suffer. And the church that was once our sanctuary is a place where we cannot speak of our struggles lest we lose the one place we have come to see as home.

Grant that our churches may become a place of healing for all the results of pain and trauma. Let it become a place where one can be as open about recovery from these addictions as from alcohol. So that, having known healing and reconciliation ourselves, we may use our recovery as a source of healing for others and Your church become a sanctuary once again for us all.

Amen

EPIDEMIC *by Stephen G. Price*
His mother asked me to tell him
what neither she nor his father could bear to say.

So I stood beside his hospital bed
and told him that both his legs were gone.

No IED had taken this vet's legs, both gone just above the knee.
They were collateral damage of a heroin overdose.
Blood supply cut off
when he passed out and woke many hours later.
They could not save the legs
nor him.

I hate the words "heroin epidemic"
because it sounds like an act of nature,
a tsunami, or the will of God
instead of the death of a young man
who brought the war home with him.

We buried him without his legs
and sang favorite songs of his, the ones
he'd liked best when Johnny Cash sang them.
There will be peace in the valley for me someday
and I fell into a burning ring of fire,
I went down, down, down and the flames went higher.
His ring of fire was fueled by pain and memory and heroin
as he searched desperately for peace in the valley.

It is not a "heroin epidemic"
that we can click past on the channels.
It is my friend, and he is dead.

COMMUNITY PRAYER

Oh Great and Grace-bestowing Gardener,
Thank you for shining a ray of peace into a chaotic jungle of obsession,
compulsion, and despair. Place your loving and skillful hands upon your
striving seedlings so that all may blossom in their own unique and blessed
varying ways. Fertilize their efforts and weed out deadly distractions on
their journey toward the Light.
Amen

+>- • -<+

QUESTIONS FOR REFLECTION/ACTION

1. Women who suffer from substance addiction and/or alcoholism are often stereotyped as lacking social character and sexual morality. How can we remove stigmas that become a deterrent to seeking recovery programs and therapy?

2. Parents with young children often put off reaching out to family or friends for help with budding addictions for fear of losing their parental rights. Can and should our tax dollars be used to create programs that serve families together, perhaps going so far as to house young families while recovery programs are being implemented?

3. How much information should be provided to children about addiction and alcoholism? How young should these discussions begin? When educational and religious programs open the doors to these discussions, should only targeted children be invited? What about children whose family situations are not easily apparent? What about teaching compassion? If it really 'takes a village,' what constitutes the village?

4. Process addictions such as shopping, gambling, and Internet use are parallel with substance addictions and yet different. How is outreach for assistance with these addictions handled in faith communities?

+>- • -<+

Jeanne Marie Westcott is a UCC Christian educator devoted to guiding children and youth in a variety of settings. She is blessed to be wife to Bruce and mother to Lillian and Grace. The extended fur-family includes Miles, Maryann, and Ginger, with guest appearances from Bueller the Snake.

8 ❋ THE CARRIER
AND THE CARRIED
REDEFINING DISABILITY

Disability is both a personal and a political reality. In the past, people with disabilities were seen as those who needed "doing for." Our lives weren't run by us, our stories weren't told by us. We were seen as the recipients of charity, not equal participants in our own communities. But we're changing that. Around the world we are now speaking with our own voices and claiming our equal right to participate. We're adding our unique perspective on what it means to be human, offering back our insights to those who have ears to hear.

Despite its pervasive nature, disability is only a portion of the person. Each one of us is less than perfect. Impairment is everywhere. But a beautiful soul can reside in any body.

PERSONAL PRAYER

THE CARRIER AND THE CARRIED *by Trish Harris*

I don't notice your disability anymore . . .
It's just something you carry with you, she said.

> I carry it with me
> like a handbag
> swinging loosely by my side
> > pick it up
> > put it down.

A handbag
I never lose
and never replace.

> I carry it on me
> like a cotton shirt
> on a summer's day.
> Wind easing its finger
> between skin and fabric
> billowing it out
> pulling at it too
> playing at separation
> but the buttons hold tight.

> I carry it in me
> channels
> carved deep
> by a river
> always in flood.

> I carry it through me
> like the weight
> of a name
> for a child never born.
> A presence
> and an absence.

> I carry it with me
> > on me
> > in me
> and through me.

> I am the carrier

> and I am also
> the carried.

> A blue tear
> filled with gold.

COMMUNITY PRAYER

God of goodness, gaps, and glitches
help us to see each other as we are.

God of struggles, strengths, and strategies
help us to cope with what we have.

God of difficulties, disabilities, and delights
help us find joy in who we are.

God of individuality and invisibilities,
enable us to understand how life is harder
for some than it is for their peers;
Give us a readiness to ease difficulties,
remove barriers, and create level
playing fields.

Bless us with the will to appreciate
the courage, creativity, and skills
required to live with an impairment;
along with the discernment to realise
impairment is merely a fragment
of personhood.

Empower us all to live in fullness,
valuing the experience we have,
and knowing we are loved.

At this time we direct our thoughts
and prayers towards those who
suffer life-blighting hidden disabilities.

As we think of those of us who are:
Crippled by accident or illness;
Deaf to the sound of voice and music;
Blind to the beauty of form and colour;
Rendered mute by malformation or disaster,
and those disabled by frailty or malfunction.

May we experience the love and care we need
and may we all be instrumental in loosening
the shackles of our dis-ease.

As we think also of those of us who are:
Blighted by ego;
Crippled by fears;
Deaf to pleadings;
Blind to injustices;
Rendered mute by apathy;
and disabled by bitterness.
May we experience the love and care we need
and may we all be instrumental in loosening
the shackles of our dis-ease. Amen

A Fable

THE TINY TOWN OF TONTEVOC—A STORY FOR CHILDREN OF ALL AGES
by Rosalie Sugrue

The tiny town of Tontevoc nestled in a sunny valley beside a sparkling
river. It was surrounded by green fields backed by snow-capped mountains. Everyone lived in a warm house, and no one went short of anything
they needed. Instead of enjoying the good things they had, though, the
children of Tontevoc School were unhappy. Each child thought some
other was more fortunate.

One child owned a pony and another had a magnificent tree house.
There was a girl who could run like the wind. Her brother could sing like
angel. Their cousins were exceptional at tennis. There were twins who
didn't look alike and often argued. A boy who painted beautiful pictures
lived with his grandmother. A family of four played boisterous games and
got to sleep in bunks. The cleverest girl in the school wore thick glasses.
Her sister was very pretty. One child lived in a grand house and had many
toys. And there was a boy who limped and had to use a crutch.

One day, the wise woman of Tontevoc visited the school holding a
bunch of floating balloons. She looked carefully at each glum face, then
instructed the children to follow her to the field behind the school. "I can

see you are dissatisfied with your lives. These balloons can help you be who you want to be." The balloons tugged on their strings as if they wanted to be free. "When you have each put your name on a balloon I will let go of the strings. While the balloons are floating you must think very carefully about what you want and who you would like to be. After a while the balloons will come down. Whichever balloon you choose to hold will become yours and you will become the person who owns that name. You will look like that child and live in that child's house and that child's family will not know you are really someone else."

As the balloons rose above the trees the children jiggled with excitement. Soon they would be pretty or clever or talented, live in a grand house or own a pony. But the balloons kept bobbing above the trees and the children kept thinking. Being in a tiny town, everyone knew something about everyone else. One father was known to get drunk. The rich girl had a nanny and seldom saw her parents. The twins got to thinking that they would miss each other terribly. The boy with the crutch thought about his baby sister who made him laugh and how his parents read bedtime stories. His grandparents, who lived next door, often showed him interesting things and they all loved each other very much.

When the balloons finally drifted downwards the children ran, frantically searching for names, and grabbing at balloons. The boy with the crutch felt a great fear. All the others could run faster than him. When he reached the last hovering balloon, oh joy of joys, it had his name on it. He looked around. The other children were clutching balloons as if their lives depended on them—and each was thinking the same thought.

Prayer

Loving God,
We acknowledge that, regardless of health,
attitude, appearance, or status,
we are people marred by imperfections.
Grant us the strength to manage our infirmities
with wise caring, good humour, and gratitude.
Help us use personal experience to become
more insightful to the conditions of other people,

and more attentive to matters spiritual.
Save us from falling victim to self-centeredness
a malaise that preys upon people of all abilities
that left unchecked is more soul destroying
and more binding than any physical condition.
In the loving of others may we find perfection. Amen

Benediction

For the God who walks on wounded feet and heals with wounded hands,
For the God who stands beside us wounded, all-knowing and all-loving,
For the God of imperfections,

ALL: We go into our wonderful and imperfect world to reflect God's perfect love,
and in so doing, claim what it is to be truly human.

→> • <←

QUESTIONS FOR REFLECTION/ACTION

1. How do we invite the insights of people with disabilities whenever issues of justice and hope are the conversation?

2. Disability and impairment are part of the human experience— what do you carry, and how are you carried?

3. How do you value all aspects of who you are?

→> • <←

Trish Harris enjoys playing with language to capture what is most difficult to say. She recently published a memoir, *The Walking Stick Tree*.

Rosalie Sugrue has the good fortune of being a fourth-generation New Zealand woman, wife, mother, and grandmother. As a retired primary school teacher she aids individuals with reading problems. As an active lay preacher she likes to push boundaries and promote the voices of the unheard.

Trish and Rosalie both have physical disabilities and met when serving on the Wellington executive council of the New Zealand Disability, Spirituality and Faith Network.

"The Carrier and the Carried" (Harris) and the "Benediction" (Sugrue) were first published in *Oh, Light*—an anthology of writings and reflections to enrich the spirit," edited by Anna Gilkinson and published by the Disability, Spirituality and Faith Network, Aotearoa New Zealand.

9 ❋ WHEN ROLES REVERSE
PARENTING PARENTS

Adult children may be called upon to care for aging parents who have diminishing physical abilities and declining memory. Sometimes children fill in as a parent when one parent dies and the other is devastated by grief, or when family relationships are strained by mental illness or substance abuse. Expectations for family care vary widely because of ethnic background, size of family, economic independence. No one can ever know the full circumstances, sacrifices, and complications of each unique family that goes through this experience. Yet we seek to honor the many portrayals of adult children parenting their mothers and fathers. Our culture often focuses on the negative aspects of these situations, ignoring the fact that many of these relationships are filled with joy.

PERSONAL PRAYER

Loving Parent, when I was a child I ran to my mother, my father for comfort in times like these. Today I come to you. This morning Mom was visiting with a lifelong friend. I watched from afar as over and over she asked, "Tell me how it is I know you." My heart broke for the one who sat patiently: answering, then redirecting, and bringing her gift of love even in the midst of sadness of lost memories.

I worry that there will be a day when Mom turns to me asking, "Tell me how it is I know you." I come to you as the one whose arms never tired of holding your children. I need to hear your voice speaking the words, "Be not afraid." Reassure me with inner peace that should a day arrive when the light of recognition fades from her face you will be there beside me. Give me the gentleness of the friend who reached out today with kindness and grace. I trust in your abiding presence.

Amen

COMMUNITY PRAYER

Loving God, Divine Parent,

We need a parent's love right now. Sometimes people call us the "sandwich generation." We who are busy tending our own children often find our parents in need of assistance with simple activities of daily life. We ask why our lives must change. We feel tired, overburdened. We look to you for wisdom.

When we tire of hearing the same old stories from forgetful parents, remind us of childhood days when a parent stood tirelessly at our side as we learned to prepare a favorite treat for the evening meal. Take us back to summer days by the lake where another endlessly baited fishhooks and cheered our first big catch, that three-inch perch. Help us remember that one who after a long day at work went with us to a concert even when it was not their favorite music, a demonstration of their love for us.

We give thanks for relationships that were marked by lifelong love and nurture. We celebrate the extended care of family and friends who stood beside us when our parents could not be there. We ask your blessings for those who chose, who choose even now to be family to us.

We pray for those whose parents were just barely enough, offering the essentials, consistently, out of duty, but grudgingly. Help us, despite the pain, to release our tendency to blame and retaliate. Give us a measure of your grace to forgive them and ourselves when we despair of the unfulfilled dreams.

Some among us rarely, if ever, knew a parent's love, but only pain and fear in the presence of unpredictable behaviors or parental absence. Grant to them a sense of healing. Inspire us to create a healing community of care that offers the nurture these your children rarely knew.

Saddened by the inability to engage shared interests of the past, help us find new connections inspired by faded snapshots of yesterday and observations from caregivers today. When we must set limits, if tempers flare or we simply have to care for other needs, help us to be gentle with ourselves. Help us to find hope in your promise of love that has no end.

We need a parent's love right now.
We give thanks that you call us each your child, your Beloved.
Amen

→→ ▪ ←←

QUESTIONS FOR REFLECTION/ACTION

1. How do we support families—parents and children—experiencing role reversal?

2. How do we honor the dignity of elders when abilities and memory decline?

3. How do we make space for people with differing family constellations and individual responsibilities?

4. How can we become more aware of the issues of teenagers caring for elders in after-school hours?

5. What resources can the church offer for healing and wholeness?

→→ ▪ ←←

Judy K. Brandon is a lover of story as told in song, poetry, quilts, gardens, and the everyday lives of people she meets at work and play. She'll gladly share stories of her three children Dre, Chris, and Jeff, who provide abundant opportunities for joy and laughter.

 I O   A TENDER LISTENING PRESENCE AT THE END OF LIFE

We all need a cloud of witnesses for our intimate choices in life, and then again in the final days before death. We need those who can laugh with us despite the pain of leaving behind everything we know to be real in this world. We need to be held in love and to be reminded of our legacy of beloved stories that will be held by others for their lifetimes. We need to work on the unfinished business of our life, while knowing that the messy business of daily life will never be resolved fully.

There are no good or bad choices about end of life care. Most nurses and nursing assistants in care facilities and hospice houses are filled with love that they share with those who have no family and may have outlived friends, whose family may live in other states or countries, those whose memories might be foggy, eroding, gone. They care not just for their patients, but also for loved ones who come to visit, concentrating on good hours and happy moments, perhaps swallowing completely and humbly the fact that they may be strangers to this cherished person.

PERSONAL PRAYER

Tender Presence

We are at home, within our familiar walls and smells
seeking peace where there is no peace . . .

hope where there seem no worldly answers . . .
but still, not in the cold noisy bustle of that sterile medical facility.

We are holding space for each other
in the kitchen where we all gathered for holiday mealtime memories,
in the shower where I now help you wash away your exhaustion,
walking haltingly together afterwards
to your side of the bed we've shared for these past fifty-seven years.
Echoes of "abide with me, and I will abide with you" sit softly beside us.
We breathe together for the time being.
Words are not always necessary,
I repeat inside my head with each struggling soul-filled breath.
Even the strongest of hearts faces the reality of that one last beat.

I was not meant for lonely sterile rooms,
but for open-windowed, quilt-comforted moments of care.
When you insist on that shower, I tell you instead,
"You know, for where I'm going, I don't really need a bath!"
I tell you slant sideways . . . I know my time is near.

"Is it imminent?" I barely whisper as you lean in ever closer . . .
On any other day, you might try weak reassurance
Holding out the doctor's false promises,
Adding a toast and a chuckle to the power of last minute miracles
But we die the way we live . . .
We don't just suddenly change how we cope.
We hold on for dear life.
Yes . . . we honestly cling to each other for dear life.

You don't know what to say . . .
We struggle silently together, letting go gently despite hope that will not die.
I am a little falling leaf
I am the song that keeps playing over and over in your head.
I am the decaying log by the shore of our lake up north . . .
where we sat for the quietly shared celebration of just one more purple
sunset.
Remembering tenderly.

COMMUNITY PRAYER

A Gathering to Openly Share Our Feelings

An occasion like this might be in a faith community or a senior center or as part of a retreat that has other topics as well. Far from being hesitant, many people long to be invited to share these concerns in a mutual setting, rather than only when a medical professional or an anxious family member conducts an "interrogation" because of a particular health issue.

We sit together, in this room bursting with God's love, to imagine our final days on this earth. Together we trust in life everlasting, and yet, we don't want our time on this earth to end. We don't want to even begin this meditation on the end of our life, even in the safety of this room full of friends. In fact, we ask, why are we even having to talk about this subject? Let's just skip this meditation and talk about our busy week ahead. No. We have come into this sacred space to share our end-of-life care hopes. We know and trust each other enough to risk being vulnerable. So sit with yourself first, and breathe. Take in the breath of life deeply and then breathe out your anxiety about approaching this time together. Quiet your heart. Then listen to your hopes.

Some people would like to listen to these questions, while others would prefer to have them written out. Please give both options.

1. Where would you like to be in your final moments of life?

2. Who would sit with you?

3. Who would you miss if they were not there with you?

4. What would you want to remember together? If you couldn't tell stories of your life, what memories would you want your loved one to recall for you?

5. Would you be comfortable being silent together?

6. What would you want to laugh about?

7. What would comfort you in your final hours?

8. What unfinished business would worry your heart?

9. What would give you hope as you face your death?

Take a few moments to sit with these questions in a place that is comfortable to you. Then write down any reflective comments that you have in your journal or just sit.

When you feel comfortable, find a trusted member of the group and share about two or three of these questions. Or share about the grief, loss, or hope that this topic brings to your heart and our time together in this small group. Remember that these are private conversations shared in the deepest of trust.

The leader should be careful that no one is left without a partner. Another choice would be to have people share by drawing names or another random fashion. One way is to give each person an index card with half a Bible verse on it and "find" the other half to become partners.

Sit quietly again, or take a walk outside with your sharing partner or alone. The world right around us has its constant reminders of the natural cycles of life and death.

This retreat is developed for people who are considering their own end time. After sharing this in a community of faith or a secular setting, consider offering a parallel experience for those who are in the time in their lives when they are helping a spouse, partner, parent, child, or friend to face these experiences.

→→ • ←←

QUESTIONS FOR REFLECTION/ACTION

1. Why do we fear death in our society?

2. In our communities of support, what actions will we take together to open up discussion of our end-of-life care hopes?

3. What would it take to develop a ministry of bereavement support?

4. What is an appropriate support ministry for both family and professional caregivers?

5. Once we have information from a retreat like this or our personal reflection, what are ways to record it and pass it on to those who might be helped in caring for us in a situation of failing health?

→► • ◄←

Carol S. Tippe is a mother, new grandmother, community health nurse of thirty-seven years, and creative compassionate caregiver at heart. She loves the words "hope" and "abide," and often settles her heart by writing poetry about her caregiving experiences. She has recently loved birthing the Bird House, a nonprofit residential hospice care home for compassionate end-of-life care.

We begin with *imago Dei*—the idea that the Divine created human beings in the Creator's own image, giving all people innate dignity, value, and worth. Within the lens of *imago Dei*, people whom both the church and society have marginalized can now see themselves as perfect, belonging and divinely created. In *imago Dei*, people who self-identify as trans (this term includes specifically transgender as well as a spectrum of other identities that go beyond the gender binary of male and female) can find a place as beloved children of the Holy One, created in the Divine's own image.

Delving into the creation story of Genesis 2, we encounter *adam* (which means "made from dirt") created in the image of the Divine. This first person was simply human and only when the Creator split *adam* in half, creating Adam and Eve, do specific genders appear. These two beings became the first expressions of male and female.

Gender, however, exists beyond these two expressions just as the spectrum of color exists beyond the three primary colors (blue, red, and yellow). When we limit our understanding or ability and don't see a whole spectrum of color or a whole spectrum of gender, we miss out on the beauty and complexity of the whole—a seemingly infinite range of shade and hue, of gender and gender expression. When we view the spectrum in its entirety, we can at last discern the fullness of the Creator's design of gender variations. Then we can know ourselves, the Holy, and all of creation more fully. The Divine invites each of us into the wholeness of the *imago Dei* with which we have been gifted, and this includes our gender identity and expression.

PERSONAL PRAYER

This poem explores the experience of identifying beyond the gender binary while seeking hope within the confines of social gender expectations. It can be used as a personal prayer for all who seek wholeness within God.

FROM HOPELESSNESS TO HOPE

Inside hopelessness—darkness,
nothing more,
impossible to be less
silence, deafening
only fears and despair
echoing off cavern walls.
I've been there, lived there
Have you? A hole so deep, so cold
No one to hear the screams—
Hopeless, alone, exhausted.
longer the stay deeper it becomes.
The darkness becomes thick—
suffocating hopes, choking dreams.
Eyes scan the darkness—
searching for light
searching for escape . . .
Hopeless.
Then it happens.
So small, almost missed
like the tide as the moon rises
darkness begins to retreat.
What is it? What is loosening the grip,

the stranglehold, the suffocating power
of darkness?
This tiny beam of light
boring its way through the thick fog
is hope.
Like an ant, small and overlooked,
carries with strength
something ten times its size,
you reach out to it, desperate to escape.
The ground slips underfoot
fearful thoughts tug at ankles
pulling deeper into the mud.
A voice, far in the distance
"stand there, stand on that rock."
Hesitantly, cautiously
obey—feet firmly planted
solid, standing tall.
Faith steadies weak knees,
raises higher, light brightens,
the darkness becomes shadows.
Still looking up, longing for a rope
a ladder, a hand
to pull up and out.
The voice calls again—"walk."
Where? you ask
I am stuck here in the hole
with the darkness eager to come back,
to strangle, to suffocate.
"Walk," you hear again,
looking down, toward the cavern wall,
a place where shadows have retreated,
where hope's rays have landed.
"Walk"—you take a step.
The rock of faith stretches out in front,

firm, supportive with each step.
Hopes shines brighter
the darkness, fringed
looking back it becomes clear.
There was never a hole, never a cavern
never an inescapable abyss.
It was only the darkness, a prison of its own.
Lifting up hands—small
radiant beams of light from your fingers
"Shine"—you hear the voice say.
"Shine"—with each step
hope shines into the dark prisons
scorching out darkness, melting cold grips
like the guard with the keys
walking an endless row of dark cells
whispering "walk," "walk."
And glancing behind—small
radiant beams of light
shine in all directions.
Soon we shall all be free
free of the despair
the silence, the loneliness,
for when we each walk
grounded on our faith
bearing our light
we become hope for others—
hope that shines, hope that encourages
hope that brightens,
so that one day, perhaps soon
the prison will be empty,
the fear will be gone,
and hope will shine upon
all whom the darkness threatens
We are the hope of our world.

COMMUNITY PRAYER

Prayer of Confession

One: Creator, Christ, and Spirit Sophia,

Many: **We confess that where you weave tapestries of interconnection and relationship, we too often look for separation, distinction, and divide.**

ONE: Where you have created rich spectrums of identity,
we pull apart only those pieces that we understand,
oppose them to each other,
and call it truth.

MANY: **Spirit and Body**
Mind and Matter
Earth and Heaven
Male and Female
Us and Them.

ONE: In so doing, we have dishonored your holy creation,
pitted ourselves against the earth and one another
and limited our own and others' ability to be our whole selves,
created in your image.

MANY: **Forgive us, Gracious One, and teach us how to see.**

ONE: Teach us to see ourselves: wise and wonderful

MANY: **Teach us to see each other: complex and nonconforming.**

ONE: Teach us to see the world: integral and interconnected.

MANY: **Teach us to see you: beyond all categories.**

ALL: **Forgive us and teach us a new way. Amen**

Words of Assurance

ONE: Friends, hear the good news.
You are created in the image of the Divine—beloved and holy.
Through Jesus Christ your sins are forgiven.
By the liberating power of the Spirit Sophia,

you are released from the bonds of category and division
freed to know and love your whole self and your neighbor
today and every day.
Amen

⇥ • ⇤

QUESTIONS FOR REFLECTION/ACTION

1. How do stereotypes or expectations around gender limit your understanding and expression of yourself?

2. How does this interpretation of the creation story challenge, shift, and expand your understanding of the creation? Of gender? Of the Divine?

3. How might you begin to expand your own and your community's imagination about the Divine and creation in terms of gender and gender identity? What resources are available to you in your community for this work?

⇥ • ⇤

Angela R. Combs has a Master of Divinity degree from Phillips Seminary and works as an independent life skills trainer for survivors of traumatic brain injuries. Angela lives in Colorado with their wife, enjoys camping and hiking, and hopes to one day earn a PhD in theology and gender studies.

Thandiwe A. Dale-Ferguson's favorite things include the color red, ice cream, taking pictures, and hiking in the mountains with her partner. Thandiwe's deep and abiding faith is nurtured by both the serious and the silly, and is lived out in her work for justice and peace in our world.

1 2 ✳ GENDER INCLUSIVITY
CHANGING LAWS,
CHANGING HEARTS

In some parts of the world, sexual and gender equality are taking root. Marriage equality is legal in more than twenty countries. Many nondiscrimination measures have expanded to include sexuality; a growing number also include gender identity. Public figures are more comfortable being "out" about their sexuality or gender identity. Within the Christian faith communities, theology and practices are becoming increasingly inclusive. More denominations are ordaining openly LGBTQ ministers, performing same-sex weddings, and baptizing children of same-sex parents. Some are revising liturgies to be inclusive of those who fall outside the gender binary, including creating name-change liturgies for people who are transitioning.

Yet jurisdictions in the United States are introducing "bathroom bills," which require individuals to use the bathroom that corresponds to the gender on their birth certificate. Nondiscrimination ordinances, especially concerning transgender people, are being repealed. Some churches are still debating the ramifications of the ordination of LGBTQ pastors. At stake, apparently, is the safety of women and children in intimate public venues like restrooms and changing spaces. At stake, apparently, is the authority of scripture and tradition.

At stake, in reality, is the maintenance of cis-hetero-patriarchy.

The concept of difference and complementarity between two genders, male and female, underlies sexism, homophobia, and transphobia. Men are seen as rational and powerful, natural leaders and protectors. Women, therefore, occupy the opposite, "complementary" categories:

emotional and vulnerable, natural nurturers in need of protection. Same-sex couples complicate this paradigm, calling into question the complementarity of, or the difference between, the sexes. Transgender people further challenge this notion by blurring the assumed link between biology—nature—and the concepts of sex and gender, as do the increasing number of people identifying with a less binary selfhood.

Recent legislation, in both public and religious spheres, seeks to uphold the old, "natural" paradigm of complementarity, despite its inherent hierarchy: assuming the powerful, almost predatory nature of men and the concurrent necessity to protect the presumably weaker women. Bathroom laws, which presume that trans women are not "real" women, but intentionally deceptive men seeking victims; the rhetoric around abortion legislation that presupposes women cannot make reasoned choices; the victim-blaming inherent in rape cases—of cis and especially trans women—remind us that sexism is prevalent in our culture. Anyone who is not a straight, cis male is disempowered—rhetorically, sexually, physically, religiously—in order to maintain the current gender hierarchy.

We cannot insist that the church is inherently different from the rest of the world and its potentially corrupt institutions, but we can hope for it to become so. The truth about sexism in the church is that the church is not only a place where sexism is tolerated, but is actively harbored and justified. Sexism in the church lives and thrives because it finds ways to ground uncritical acquiescence to sexism on biblical and theological bases. The church is not immune to rape culture. In fact, it has been and continues to be a bastion of it. Its responses to abuse and violence against women, including dismissiveness towards victims and an emphasis on submission, prove this. Its lack of response to the frequent violence against trans women dehumanizes and blames the victims, a heartbreaking response from an institution that professes to stand in solidarity with the marginalized.

Sexism, homophobia, and transphobia are manifestations of our human brokenness, our human propensity to find ways to exert power over the other. Sexism, homophobia, and transphobia are a manifestation of sin, defined as separation from God and the rejection of the emancipatory power of God's love.

Sexism triumphs by abbreviating our imagination for what the church—both members and leaders—are called to do and be. It thrives on setting restrictive parameters for our identity, limits to our abilities, and restrictions to our own potential. It is fully aware of our struggle to embody our true selves, especially when those selves are already devalued by a gendered hierarchy, and looks for any crack in the surface by which to replace authenticity with illusion. Sexism, homophobia, and transphobia deny the power of God to work through all members of God's creation. They shape a God in the image of our patriarchal human culture—an idol that the church has too long worshiped.

It need not be so. The church can again be the community where the women first proclaimed the resurrection. We can be the safe place for those excluded from their families. We can be the people who see injustice, grief, and loss, and who strive to bring about healing and wholeness, for the entire body of Christ.

PERSONAL PRAYER

Holy one, open my heart, that I may understand clearly the injustices of this world:

the blame placed on victims of sexual or gender-based violence
the small number of women in positions of political
and economic power
the words used to disempower and silence women:
bossy, shrill, bitch
the assumption that gays and lesbians are pedophiles
the narrative of the "deceptive trans person" as sexual predator
the policing of women's appearances
the insistence that trans people "pass"
the high rate of violence against the LGBTQ community,
    especially trans women of color
the acceptance without protest that 41percent of trans people
attempt suicide
        because of a lack of specific mental health resources
the congregations who require LGBTQ members to change or leave
the theology that leads to physical and emotional abuse and violence.

Abiding God, break me open to the pain of the body of Christ;
and by your Spirit, work in me to lift up the voices of the voiceless
encourage me to empower the powerless
and to say with confidence in your grace:
not in the name of my God.

COMMUNITY PRAYER

Litany of Repentance

God of love, we confess that we are in bondage to a view of the world that puts our compromise before your justice; that is unable to name the worth and wonder of all of your children; that places people in positions that threaten the very soul of who they are—the soul that you see as unique and glorious.

We confess that, all too often, we perpetuate the sins of the church, unwilling to tell the truth of the ways in which even those who call upon your name do so for the sake of harm.

We ask for your forgiveness. We pray for wholeness. We trust in the promise of your hope. Grant us, we pray, the courage to speak, the power to empower, the mercy to love.
Amen

Assurance of Grace

God frees us and it is uncomfortable; God frees us that it makes us responsible to witness and to act. God frees us with a formidable forgiveness.

⤜ • ⤛

QUESTIONS FOR REFLECTION/ACTION

1. In what ways have you experienced to sexism in our culture? In the church? Has that ever caused you to speak out, to bear witness?
2. How might your congregation be more supportive of those who have traditionally been disempowered by a patriarchal culture?

3. How can local churches or denominational entities engage culture on behalf of those who are disempowered or even outcast?

⤙ • ⤚

Karoline M. Lewis is the Marbury E. Anderson Chair in Biblical Preaching at Luther Seminary in St. Paul, Minnesota. She is the author of *John* in the Fortress Biblical Preaching Commentaries and *SHE: Five Keys to Unlock the Power of Women in Ministry.*

Eliza Buchakjian-Tweedy is the senior pastor of First Church Congregational, United Church of Christ in Rochester, New Hampshire. She is a contributing writer for the RevGal-BlogPals collective, as well as for Fidelia's Sisters, the publication of the Young Clergy Women Project.

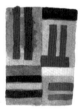

13 ✳ DISMANTLING RACISM
THE POWER OF PRIVILEGE

In 2013 when Trayvon Martin, a young unarmed black man, was killed by a man who was not held accountable for his death, people used social media to bring his story beyond the black community, and the #Black LivesMatter movement came into being. In 2014, when unarmed teenager Michael Brown was shot and killed by a police officer in his community and left on a Ferguson street for hours without judicial consequence, the movement grew stronger. Since 2015, the movement has become international. This new civil (human) rights movement is largely being led by youth. Some have even heard it remarked that it has given them hope that they have not felt before.

Racism is insidious and is so much part of the fabric of society that we can become unaware of its existence. The truth is that racism won't just go away. It must be consciously dismantled. It exists around the world wherever people are redefined as *us* and *them*. Skin color is an easy identifier but there are other dividers. The underlying concern is the dehumanization of persons in order to allow hatred to fester.

It is very easy to hate, distrust, and blame *them*, especially when *they* may be seen as less than human—less deserving of love, caring, equal existence, equal rights, or respect—and destroyed without remorse. The problem with this thinking, of course, is that we are all part of God's creation. When someone is killed or hurt we are all diminished. The damage (trauma) may be physical, emotional, spiritual, or psychological.

The work of reconciliation and antiracist groups is about recognizing and acknowledging the privilege, the unspoken power structure that assigns differing value to persons, allowing some to benefit from the oppression and devaluation of the other. Racism damages not only the oppressed and oppressor but is toxic to society as a pervasive evil. Only when privilege is acknowledged and persons are valued as children of God can change happen and justice prevail.

PERSONAL PRAYER

O great Creator, you know and love each of your children intimately and have given each person life and promise. I ache as I hear of each young person snuffed out as if they were no more than insects. It is especially painful if it is at the hands of those who are supposed to protect. I cry for the families who must bury their loved one, a child, a spouse, a friend, and find no justice in systems that tolerate and even support the killer.

Why is there fear of dark skin? Why is there such hatred in the world for those who are different?

You, O Compassionate One, love and care for each person.
In your eyes, every life is cherished,
these black lives matter to you,
the lives of the hated and despised matter to you,
the lives of the oppressed matter to you.
You hurt when we hurt. None of us is outside your love.

O God, let me first see the human being, a creature into which you blew your own life.

Let me see the beauty of that person in the variety of colors, hair textures, personalities, thoughts, and abilities that you have bestowed on humankind. It is the beauty of your life within them, their spark of divinity, I want to see. We are all yours, which makes it impossible to dismiss, discard, deem unimportant or irrelevant any group of people. Let me cast aside any feelings of unworthiness I myself hold.

I pray that I may always see others through your eyes. If I see that persons are dehumanized, help me to speak up for them. Give me courage to stand in solidarity with those who have no voice. Let me feel your presence as I move through the world so that I may not ignore or remain unmoved by injustice.

I pray for those who disregard or dismiss the problems people of color must endure. Let them open their hearts to recognize the injustice that they themselves perpetuate through their denial. Let them truly comprehend the issues and act with justice.

I pray for these who hate, fear, and kill, that they might find some sense of the damage they do not only to the victim and their family but to the community, society, and themselves. God, please help people see all other people with love rather than with hate or fear.

> O God of Love
> I ask you to heal my broken heart
> with your expansive love. Let love flow
> through me that I may help heal the brokenness
> caused by racism. Turn my anguish into the
> power of love so that I may be counted as
> one drop in an ocean of drops that
> transforms the world as we
> know it into the world
> as you know it
> can be.
> Amen

COMMUNITY PRAYER
Litany

ONE: In the past, black people were lynched or attacked by dogs.

MANY: **Did black lives matter?**

ONE: Today they are shot and left to die.

MANY: **Do black lives matter?**

ONE: One is choked, one is shot, one is knocked around in the back of a van and no medical care is rendered.

MANY: Will black lives matter?

ONE: A person is killed and people blame the victim.

MANY: Do black lives matter?

ONE: Brown, black, red, yellow skin lead some to senseless fear, but we know we are made in your image, O God.

MANY: Black lives *do* matter!

ONE: We are one body in Christ, and individually members one of another.

MANY: Black lives matter. Help us to realize that all lives matter only when black lives matter.

Communion

We are invited to God's table. Jesus welcomed everyone to the dismay of the religious leaders of the day. It was clear that to Jesus, station in life did not prevent one from receiving God's love and grace. Even perceived sinfulness was not a criterion for exclusion.

Today we come to this table with insidious toxic racism permeating the fabric of society in so many places on earth. Often we are unaware of it. Some try to be conscious of the problem but still benefit from it. Some are in denial; some simply don't care. But it damages us all.

Jesus says, "You are welcome as you are, beloved of God." We must likewise show extravagant welcome to everyone. So come to the table, all you who need love and comfort, guidance, support, and forgiveness. God's grace is abundant and can be found at this table where we are all wanted, accepted, and loved.

→→ • ←←

QUESTIONS FOR REFLECTION/ACTION

1. What underlies the inability (or refusal) to say, "Black lives matter"? Does it call for an argument or a change of heart?

2. How can one avoid the dehumanization trap?

3. What do you think Jesus would have to say about racism, given his understanding of God's love for all humankind?

⤞ • ⤝

Devoree Clifton Crist, MD, is a spiritual director who received a Master of Theology from Eden Theological Seminary and Graduate Certificate in Spiritual Direction from Acquinas Institute of Theology. Her work is primarily with individuals, but she has an active retreat ministry and works with groups. Her roots are in the Roman Catholic Church and she now worships and serves in the Christian Church (Disciples of Christ), where she is chair of the Commission on Mission and Unity and on the pro-reconciliation/antiracism team for the region. She is multiracial, is married, and has two adult children. Music and art are very much a part of her ministry.

14 CULTURAL DIVERSITY
LOVING EVERY ELEMENT OF IT, FOR GOD'S SAKE

We are called to love our neighbors as we love ourselves, but are we truly willing to love with full acceptance? Do we really believe that we are all different but equal before the eyes of our Creator? Does acceptance and tolerance equal love? Acceptance is not enough. Tolerance is not enough. While tolerance may seem like an improvement over hate or animosity, and acceptance seems closer to loving that tolerance, the critical step on the road from tolerance to acceptance to love is respect. Respect is crucial, and honoring the integrity of others is vital on our way to love.

I recall visiting a university town whose residents prided themselves on their diversity. They considered it a reflection of their values and intelligence. These were good people, many of them people of faith. They were smart and community-minded. They were also mostly white middle-class Americans.

A diverse community is not in people's claim of themselves, but in the sincerity of their actions to create a place of love for all people. It is developed in cooperation regardless of differences. It is found when those whose identities grant them disproportionate power sit at the feet of neighbors and listen to their stories. It evolves when everyone perceives the integrity of others simply because of their humanity.

It has been suggested that a community is only diverse when no group has a majority. True as that might be, it does not excuse people in other settings from doing the work of understanding and love. Those of us who often experience the privileges of the majority have much to learn from our neighbors. Those of us who belong to nondominant groups have much to teach. However, the responsibility to learn is greater than the responsibility to teach, and it is simply a continuation of injustice for those with power to expect those with less to do the work of educating. If in our lives we have done work in ourselves and in our community that makes it worth another's time to tell us their stories, may we have the wisdom to listen. May we all learn and teach as it blesses us.

PERSONAL PRAYER*

Thank you. I'm sorry.

I need to say both. Thank you to everyone who has written, sung, or spoken the difficult truths of discrimination, oppression, and privilege. Thank you to my friends who have taken the time to tell me their stories so that I might understand my own history better, so that I might understand myself better. I'm sorry that you have these painful stories to tell. I regret that I didn't already know them. I realize now that I've been callous about your experience and ignorant of my own privilege. I apologize for those times when I've relied on you to teach me about oppression rather than take responsibility for learning it myself.

Thank you and I'm sorry.

The Rev. Dr. Martin Luther King Jr. wrote in his "Letter from Birmingham Jail," "Injustice anywhere is a threat to justice everywhere. We are caught in an inescapable network of mutuality, tied in a single garment of destiny. Whatever affects one directly, affects all indirectly."

If he is right, then I cannot understand the garment of my own life without knowing more of yours. To the extent that I have earned your trust to hear your story, I'm grateful. To the extent that I have not earned your trust, I hope to be humble and faithful. To the extent we may never fully trust one another enough to bear fully one another's stories, God, hold us in your grace.

When I do not see my own privilege—open my eyes.
When I do not hear the cries of my neighbors—open my ears.
When I do not acknowledge my own complicity in unjust systems—
open my heart.
When I see privilege excused, give me courage to speak.
When I hear discrimination pardoned, give me faith to act.
When I find oppression allowed, give me love to build a new reality.
Please, dear God.

COMMUNITY PRAYER

Creator of the diverse universe,
you have given us a responsibility.
We pray for your wisdom
to help us challenge the status quo.

Creator of the diverse universe,
help us to no longer accept or tolerate,
but honor the integrity of one another,
simply because of our humanity.

Creator of the diverse universe,
help us destroy fear, which paralyzes us
causing the drape of exclusivity
to cover our eyes.

Creator of the diverse universe,
we pray that you help us understand
that we are all members of your family,
and we are all called to your table.

Creator of the diverse universe,
forgive us for forgetting
to love unconditionally,
which transcends all and does all.

Creator of the diverse universe,
help us to take the steps

to both learn and teach
honor, integrity, justice, and peace.

Creator of the diverse universe,
help us remove the blinders of indifference
to live in solidarity, appreciating our differences,
for sameness was never part of the plan.

We are members of
your blessed creation;
blessed we are, blessed we are.
Amen

→‣ ● ◂←

QUESTIONS FOR REFLECTION/ACTION

1. To what extent do you consider yourself all-loving and all-inclusive?
   If you are honest with yourself, what "category" of people are
   hardest for you to include? (members of the Ku Klux Klan,
   pedophiles, teenagers who can't stop looking at their phones)

2. How far does your definition of diversity stretch? Go ahead and
   write it out!

3. What restricts you from fully exemplifying our Creator's love for
   humanity?

4. What one action can you take today to show trust and help build
   the beloved community? Okay, what about tomorrow?

*The personal prayer written by Susan Phillips was originally published in a blog
on Patheos.*

→‣ ● ◂←

Luz Berrios-Taveras, fondly known as Lucy, is a lay member and secretary of the board of New Creation Ministries, a partnership of the United Church of Christ and the Evangelical Lutheran Church in America (ELCA) in Manchester, Connecticut. Lucy has been married to her husband Orlando for twenty-two years and together they have two children.

Susan Phillips is a child of God, called and blessed, convicted and forgiven, mama, spouse, servant, trying to be a disciple. She pastors First Presbyterian Church, Shawano, Wisconsin, and practices interfaith dialogue with her family and talks to strangers. She is a worship designer and workshop leader at FaithfulSpaces.com.

15 GUN VIOLENCE AND GUN CONTROL IN THE UNITED STATES

The United States is a nation marked by a strong prevalence of gun ownership among its citizenry, a culture of the "right" for its citizens to bear arms that is steeped in certain interpretations of its very Constitution, and an enduring narrative of seemingly any frontier—geographic or figurative—being conquerable with the aid of firearms.

There are those who own guns they use to hunt for food to feed their families or pursue the shooting sports, and most gun control advocates respect these uses. Yet even in the midst and wake of numerous mass shootings and the reality that on average seven children and teens under the age of twenty each day are killed by gun violence in the United States, an intractable struggle persists between gun-rights and gun-control advocates.

PERSONAL PRAYER

My heart aches, O God, for another child, another image of you, caught in the crossfire. Oh—my—God, the *crossfire*. Why has that word never struck me like this before? The cross-fire. Your cross: a symbol of your self-giving love. Your fire: a symbol of your Holy Spirit. How can I bring your cross and your fire to bear on this duel, this showdown, this shootout?

I need the breadth and depth of your love, so starkly and hauntingly depicted on a crude Roman cross, to enter more deeply into the reasons one might choose to have a gun. What causes anyone to be so terrified, so enraged, so entitled? What of the sport of it? Must one form of hunting inevitably lead to all other forms of hunting? What of the previously assaulted, the previously hunted? What of those targeted by the state, or empire—just like you, Jesus?

I need your fire, the fire of your Holy Spirit, to ignite my passion for justice, for life, for children, for hope. Maybe I can "fight fire with fire" after all: your fire, the fire *of* justice, the fire *of* life, the fire *of* children, the fire *of* hope.

Between your cross and your fire is resurrection; resurrection and stories of seeing you along the way, especially in the breaking of bread. Death is not final. Death is not final. Death is not final. Not even the death dealing of a gun-drenched America. That is the story of my faith. Is not this faith, my faith in you, a faith to stand in the crossfire?

If I choose to stand in the crossfire, what will I feel, what will I say, what will I do?
    I will feel afraid and vulnerable and open.
    I will say that you came to give us life, not to take life away.
    I will do something I never thought I could do before.

    I will rise.

I will rise to the challenge. I will rise to enter the story. I will rise to a new level of conversation with those whose opinions are diametrically opposed to mine. I will rise to a different experience of your cross. I will rise in the heat and flame of your fire: the fire *of* justice, the fire *of* life, the fire *of* children, the fire *of* hope.

Walk with me, Jesus. Walk with me into the crossfire. Amen

COMMUNITY PRAYER

Dodging Bullets: A Sequence of Reconciliation

Call to Reconciliation

In all our dodging and weaving, God waits for us to stand still, catch our breath, and cry out for healing and grace.

Prayer of Confession

Howling, Horrified God of Hope,

Too many children—our children, *your* children—are becoming far too adept at dodging bullets—in their streets, their alleys, their parks, their schools, their homes.

How ironic that dodge ball is considered too dangerous to be sanctioned play at recess while dodging bullets has become a necessary life skill for children in these United States of America.

From our urban jungles, to our amber waves of grain, to our suburban sanctuaries, our school children learn lockdown routines to prepare them for the possibility of an armed intruder.

In a mad rush to protect ourselves from anyone and everyone—but ourselves—many of our homes now house more guns than human lives.

How is it that we see no contradiction in praying with Isaiah "to turn our swords into ploughshares and our spears into pruning hooks," while arming ourselves at the rate of nine guns for every ten people, including children?

Unhinge our hearts, O God, from this culture of violence and prison of extreme self-reliance, that we may dig deeper than the nearest holster or pocket or pocketbook or pillow or gun cabinet to consider what we are most desperately dodging: fear, self-doubt, trauma, meaninglessness.

You, Holy One, have the power to make all things new—even here, even now, even us.

Open then our hearts to the power and presence of your steadfast love. Teach us your ways of peace and reconciliation, with one another and ourselves. Embolden us to lay down our arms that we may teach your still more excellent way to our children, *your* children, in hope and in peace. Amen

Assurance of Grace

God's grace and reconciliation makes all things new: even here, even now, even us. Thanks be to God.

⇥ • ⇤

QUESTIONS FOR REFLECTION/ACTION

1. Do you currently own or have you ever owned a gun?

2. If not, seek out someone who does, arrange a face-to-face meeting, and ask that person to help you understand why she or he chooses to own one. If you have or do, seek out someone who never has, arrange a face-to-face meeting, and ask that person to help you understand why he or she chooses not to own one.

3. Why do you think the United States has such high gun ownership rates, especially compared to other developed countries?

4. How does your understanding of Jesus' teaching and actions as we encounter them in the gospels support or challenge your own position on gun rights and gun control?

⇥ • ⇤

Shelly Davis is a pastor, preacher, and poet living and serving in Milton, Massachusetts. She prays and works for the day when none of God's children will believe they need a gun.

16 ✳ STANDING UP FOR AN INCLUSIVE, JUSTICE-SEEKING GOD

The voices are not just in my head. They shout from the front page of the newspaper. They scream from the cover of a news magazine. They preach from the newsfeed on my laptop. They are not new voices, but echo Lamentations in psalms and prophecies.

Why is God letting this happen?

Why doesn't God do something?

Why does such cruelty exist in a world God created and deemed good?

False prophets reflect on tragic events—events of horror, spawned by evil—and declare that an angry god is lashing out to punish and obliterate such sinners. Can we, as children of a loving God, counter these voices? How do we, as people of a grieving God, speak the truth to silence these voices? How do I pray? Whom do we worship? How do we stand up and proclaim a welcoming justice-seeking God?

PERSONAL PRAYER

Abba, I open my heart to you. Search me. See any darkness lurking in my soul. Shine your light on it. Help me to see, to name, and to wrestle with the evil we find. Surround my weakness with your strength. Hold the broken bits of me in your embrace. Heal and soothe the fractures in my spirit.

Then give me the courage to seek the evil in the spaces around me. Help me to shine your light into the dark corners of this world. Give me the strength to gently hold the wounded that I encounter. Together, with others who would include rather than discard, may we work for a beloved community. Together, with others who would heal rather than wound, may we find your balm in Gilead. Together, with those who would speak love rather than cry out vengeance, may we take responsibility for tragedy and silence the voices of discord.

May your peace and justice begin within me. May your healing and grace begin with my words. May your light of love and compassion begin with my work for your realm.
Amen

COMMUNITY PRAYER

Litany

God of justice and mercy,
Where there is bigotry,
    let us envision love.
Where we hear cruelty,
    let us speak kindness.
Where we see injustice,
    let us act with righteousness.
Where we lose justice,
    let us find mercy.
Facing the brokenness of this world,
    we ask for courage to seek your healing.
When the money changers fill your temple,
    let our anger be righteous and directed toward building your realm.
This morning—and every morning that we draw breath—we ask for strength to be your voice
    as we speak truth to power
as we envision compassion and equity
    as we seek your justice, your mercy, and your peace.

⤞ • ⤝

QUESTIONS FOR REFLECTION/ACTION

1. Whom do I know who is hurting today? What one small, kind deed may I do for this person?

   Action: Call, visit, write a note to someone who needs to hear a voice of comfort. (Yes, get in your car and visit that member of your congregation who has been housebound!)

2. What evil do I see splayed across my path? What one word of justice may I speak?

   Action: Find an issue of injustice (racial tensions, LGBTQ oppression, child exploitation) and connect with an organization working to make change. (Yes, go on the Internet and find a local organization that can use your time and money!)

3. What voice do I hear spewing divisiveness and hatred? What one prayer of grace may I put in its path?

   Action: Do not let the voices of false prophets go unanswered. Take one voice (politicians who demonize groups of people, preachers who use scripture to enforce ungodly ideas), and craft or find words to change the direction of the discussion. (Yes, practice words of justice and peace and then speak them when you hear those voices in public places. Be willing to be confrontational as Jesus confronted those who defiled God's sanctuary!)

⤞ • ⤝

LL Kroouze DuBreuil is the pastor of Faith United Church of Christ in Union, New Jersey. A native of Bristol, Pennsylvania, Dr. DuBreuil is a life-long advocate for peace and social justice. In addition to her seminary work, she has degrees in education and theater and has worked in the public schools of New Jersey, regional theaters, and business—all of which she puts to good use in her role as pastor. Her two essential strengths are righteous anger and a sense of humor.

17 SOLDIER'S HEART
REACHING OUT TO VETERANS AND THEIR FAMILIES

Veterans come in a spectrum of ages, colors, gender identities, and sexual orientations, as well as levels of wellness and woundedness. Veterans and their families encounter many deep spiritual challenges, including the loss and stress involved in changing homes and schools every few years, the fear and anxiety of having a spouse or parent stationed far away for months at a time, and the struggles for acceptance and support in a country that is ambivalent in its treatment of vets.

For many combat veterans, spiritual challenges run even deeper. Their condition, once called "soldier's heart" or "shell shock," and now called PTSD, involves not just physical but emotional and spiritual woundings as well. The resources here may help faith communities, individual caregivers, and family and friends assist veterans to find some of the healing they need in their lives.

PERSONAL PRAYER

Deployment

It is difficult for any serviceperson to handle deployment. If married, they worry about their spouse's well-being. If parents, they worry about how their children will fare. Their family members and friends worry about their safety. Here are two prayers, one for a child whose parent is away, the other for a family whose member is leaving.

Dear God,
You know how scared _____ is right now. You know her/his mom/dad
is in _____ , where there is a war. Please protect _____ (parent) and
bring her/him home safely. And please help _____ remember that
_____ loves her very much, and that you do, too. Amen

Dear God,
We pray for this family as _____ leaves to go to _____. Please keep
them safe while they are apart. Give them courage and patience as they
wait. Help them all remember how much they love each other, and keep
fresh in their hearts good memories of their very best times together. Let
them look forward to the day when _____ comes home, when they
will celebrate together. Amen

Coming Home

*Vets returning home often suffer feelings of estrangement from their families and
friends, anxiety about building their lives anew, and residual trauma from their
military experiences, especially if they served in combat.*

I just got home, God—and everything is strange.
I still hear gunfire, still smell fear and sweat and blood, still see horrors.
Quiet me, God. Heal me, Holy One.
Help me unclench, and open my heart and arms to those I love.
Help us, together, become family again.
Amen

Finding a Home

*Vets make up one-fourth of the homeless population. On any given night, some
two hundred thousand of them have no safe shelter, no food security. Homeless
women vets may face additional challenges as single mothers or as survivors of
military sexual trauma. May we both pray and work together so that all veterans
may have a safe place to live.*

O God, we pray for warm, safe places—
    with clean floors, a chair for sitting, bright bed-quilts,
    and doors to close and lock out dangers,
for (this veteran) and for all your children.

We pray for good food on the table, each and every meal.
We pray, God, that (this veteran) will find friendship and
support in this community,
    and help in growing a new sense of home here.
And we pray, God, that you use all of us so that veterans are honored
and cared for
    when they return from serving their country.
Amen

In the Hospital

After twenty-five-plus years of visiting vets in the hospital, I've learned that veterans' hospitals vary widely in their conditions and services. What seldom varies is how lonely so many of the patients feel. Some have lost their families because of the stresses of their military service. Some have outlived their comrades. Many feel abandoned by their country and their God.

The grizzled vet, iron-gray cheeks stubbled or downy,
    scars visible and invisible,
lies in bed
in a plain gray room
with concrete-block walls.

He waits . . . for the doctor's daily visit,
    for a nurse to take his vitals (and touch him . . . oh, human contact),
for the lunch-cart (will there be ice-cream today?).

She hopes . . . for just one visitor today,
    maybe a friend with a good joke, or
    a chaplain to wheel her out to the garden, so she can feel sunlight
    on her skin.

In spite of pain . . . loneliness . . . they have not given up.
They still seek hope.

And so, O God, hold this child of yours tenderly. Wait with him. Be with her in the visit of a friend. Touch them with the hands of loving caregivers. And always, help this brave one know, you are here. Amen.

COMMUNITY PRAYER

ONE: On this day, O God, we celebrate the many gifts of freedom.

MANY: **Freedom from old prejudices, old hatreds, old ways of thinking
that separate us from our sisters and brothers,
freedom from hardships and constraints that so many live with,
freedom to stop, and begin again, this time on your path.**

ONE: On this day, Holy God, we give thanks for those who
have worked, served, sacrificed in the service of their country's ideals,
that others might be free.

MANY: **We thank you for the men and women who serve or have served
in our military forces. And we ask that you bless them.**

ONE: We thank you, God, for those whose consciences led them to serve in
ways other than as combatants, working on behalf of their communities
to create peace and justice at home.

MANY: **We give thanks for their faith commitments and their service.
And we ask that you bless them.**

ONE: We also lift up, honor, and celebrate the families of those who have
worked, served, and fought for freedom.

MANY: **We pray for those who held their families together while loved
ones served far away, for those whose loved ones never returned, and for
those still working to heal their families as loved ones do come home.
And we ask that you bless them.**

ONE: Gracious God, we pray that you keep all these in your care this
day. And we pray that as we honor them, we might rededicate ourselves
to your service, praying and working for peace, in our nation, and for
all nations.

MANY: **We offer these prayers in the name of Jesus, our Christ, and
Prince of Peace. Amen**

⤜ ● ⤛

QUESTIONS FOR REFLECTION/ACTION

1. What are the needs of veterans in your community? How can you learn more about them? Is there a way to ask veterans themselves rather than turning to online resources?

2. What resources does your congregation have to help address these needs? Some of these may be volunteer time, space, money, energy, advocacy. Stretch your imagination—don't stop at your first answer.

3. With whom can you partner so you can be more effective?

➤➤ • ◂◂

Sharyl B. Peterson is a UCC pastor in the process of retiring after twenty-five years in ministry. She is getting ready to spread her wings as community storyteller, poet, hospice volunteer, and maker of artists' books. And she is trying to stay open to the new possibilities that retirement will bring.

18 ✻ MEETING JESUS
HUMAN RIGHTS BEHIND BARS

Jesus tells us in Matthew 25 that one of the standards for the judgment of faithfulness is "I was in prison and you visited me." We're told that each time we reach out to those who are incarcerated, we are, in fact, reaching out to Jesus. It is often difficult to see Jesus in the faces of persons who have committed serious or heinous crimes; but Jesus did not add a footnote. Nor did he say, when he preached at Nazareth, that he came only to free those who were unjustly charged or guilty of minor offenses. The passage he quotes from Isaiah 61:1 speaks of "telling the captives and prisoners they have been set free . . . and to bind up the brokenhearted."

It becomes our task to address these broken ones in such a way that the safety of victims is maintained, and that the lives of offenders are changed. We must let our hearts be broken for the victimized one in every offender before we can find the wisdom and courage to seek new ways of addressing the offender in the here and now. And we also remember that there are those who are incarcerated who are innocent. We respond to them all.

PERSONAL PRAYERS

A MOTHER'S LAMENT

They shut you away today
Your broken spirit

Weighing heavily under the weight of a guilty verdict—and what you
have done

You will serve your time
    within prison walls, with guards and bars and constant scrutiny
    until released in someone else's clothes with your bag of possessions
    to move into a 10 x 10 room on the third floor of a rooming house
        with oppressive heat and shivering cold and bed bugs
        allowed only to go for food, appointments
            a job—if you can get one
            counseling—if there is any
        and subject to invasive searches of your room and your soul
            for something—"I know you are doing something"
            to send you back to prison

And when your ten years are over, you will spend the rest of your life
subject to
    angry judgments dismissing you
        from social interactions
        from family celebration
        from public gatherings, including church
        left alone to continue imprisonment forever

UNLESS
you believe your God when God promises eternal love, grace,
and forgiveness

Then—and only then—will you be able to thrive in spite of
others' judgments
        as I, your mother
        weep and pray, curse and worry
        yearning for your resurrection, my resurrection,
        others' resurrections
        separated by miles and restrictions and crippling fear
        yet sustained by faith in God's gifts of hope and joy and peace
        and love

GOD IS A MOTHER

God is a mother
visiting her son in prison.
Every Saturday
she mounts the steps of the Greyhound bus
and rides the 3 ½ hours
out of the city and into the country
past the cornfields and alfalfa and razor wire
through the metal detector and the sally port
to sit in the Visiting Room and wait
til it suits someone to let him come down.
God is a mother
visiting her son in prison,
her hair going grey, then white, over the years
as she carries her paper bag
with sandwich and soda
to eat in the waiting room.
O love that will not let me go,
God is a mother
visiting her son in prison.

LETTER FROM A MOTHER TO A SON IN PRISON

Oh that I could board a bus
Or drive every other weekend when you are allowed visitors
1200 miles—so many miles—imprison me and keep me from your side

I must be content with your collect calls to our landline whenever
Keeping me close to the phone, so not to miss a call

Oh that I could be transported to your side
Be with you in your confinement
And comfort you as I did when you fell off of your bike
    fought with a friend, failed a test, or felt alone

The miles, the rules, the restrictions, the angry responses of fear, of family
imprison me

COLLATERAL INMATES

They come every week;
Saturdays mostly,
sometimes Sunday.
They step off the bus that drives them to the gate
or park old cars, often borrowed
from friends or parents
in the lot where toddlers and small children
tumble out of vehicles
like dice from a shaken cup.
Young mothers with babies on breast or hip
sullen teens pulled away from weekends
elderly parents, faces lined with shame.
Inmates come to visit inmates.
Sometimes
if it weren't for the glass partition
and the regulation dress code,
just looking at the faces
you couldn't tell
who will go home when the visiting hours are over
and who will go back to the cell block

COMMUNITY PRAYER

PRAYER FOR INMATES

O God, bless our sons and daughters, our mothers and fathers, our brothers and sisters, as they walk this path. Keep them close, help them feel your presence in every lonely hour in spite of the limitations that are the result of society's fear of those convicted of a crime.

O God, grant me courage, strength, and openness to work through this raging anger at the system, at family members, at society, when they judge and dismiss and throw us and those we love away.

Resurrect us in your spirit, in your love, in your just and faithful way, that we may live and move and be all that you create us to be. Amen

PRAYER FOR EMPLOYEES AND VOLUNTEERS OF CORRECTIONAL FACILITIES
by Maren Tirabassi

God, bless my poetry circle today
so that new inmates join us
as well as familiar friends.
Bless his basketball team,
and another one's GED program.
Bless the new cook
trying to learn how to meet the
religious food needs of our folks,
and bless the program for inmates
recording bedtime stories for their kids.
Bless the guard who is becoming cynical,
the volunteer who is forgetting
her boundaries, the advocate for
immigration concerns,
the new hire on the desk,
trying to act like he's tough
and being too mean to the visitor
who didn't read the dress code.
Bless the warden who tries so hard
the chaplain who prays so hard,
the therapist who won't give up,
and all the 12 steppers
selling serenity, courage, and wisdom,
because we need all three. Amen

→► ● ◄←

QUESTIONS FOR REFLECTION/ACTION

1. Where do you receive impressions of correctional institutions—
   from personal visits and friends or relatives who have experienced
   them or from movies and television shows? Why are those very different sources of information?

2. Why do you think that people sometimes reoffend and return to prison? Is your faith community open and welcoming to those who have served sentences in prison?

3. What kinds of support groups are available in your community for families of people who are incarcerated?

→→ • ←←

Stephen G. Price is the interim pastor of First Baptist Church Hyattsville in Maryland. He and his wife, Carole, have five children and four grandchildren between them. They love to kayak together.

Barbara Wass VanAusdall's career teaching second language speakers who came to the states escaping injustice, discrimination, and abuse, as well as local students caught in difficult situations, sensitized her to injustices that could not be ignored. She addressed them in class projects and in shared conversations and activities with students. She continues to do so as a retiree through her music and writings, work as a lay minister, and issues in her own family.

19 ❋ AUTHORIZED VIOLENCE
THE MILITARIZATION OF POLICE

We live in very difficult times. On the news we see people gathered for a peaceful protest confronted by police officers wearing helmets, masks, and "riot gear" while carrying assault weapons. Later in the same newscast, during the sports segment, people can often be seen setting cars on fire, turning over furniture, and getting into fights. They are described as "celebrating" their team victory while uniformed police stand by. There is a difference in the way the police prepare to "protect and serve" different communities.

Some communities equip their police departments with weapons that are designed to be used in a war. These weapons are in the hands of police officers who are generally fearful of people who do not look like them or people who they have been taught to perceive as inherently dangerous. These officers are prepared to kill and destroy the enemy, except the "enemy" is our neighbor. Heavily armed police escalate fearful responses in civilians. Fear begets fear. Armed fear often results in death of unarmed civilians. Such excessive force by police is particularly disturbing given its disproportionate impact on people of color. It's deeply troubling when the police see themselves at war with the community rather than as public servants who are responsible for community safety.

The systems we live with are flawed. Racism, sexism, heterosexism/homophobia, transphobia, ageism, ableism, and many other "isms" people experience shape our understanding of the world in which we live and move. As people of faith, we are called to imagine that a different world is possible and then live in such a way as to make it possible. Our world is flawed, but every time a child laughs, there is hope for peace and justice.

On July 13, 2013, George Zimmerman was acquitted for fatally shooting Trayvon Martin, an unarmed seventeen-year-old African American young man on his way home from a convenience store in Florida. George Zimmerman, a neighborhood watch volunteer, used the "stand your ground" law in Florida as his defense for shooting the young man he did not recognize who was wearing a hooded sweatshirt ("hoodie") and carrying Skittles and Arizona Ice Tea. That evening, as the verdict was announced, three African American queer women—Alicia Garza, Patrisse Cullors, and Opal Tometi—began talking with each other on Facebook and Twitter. Alicia Garza wrote a Facebook post titled "A Love Note to Black People" in which she wrote: "Our Lives Matter, Black Lives Matter." The other two responded with what was a simple hashtag: #blacklivesmatter. People began using the hashtag and telling their own stories, and people who do not understand the need for self-affirmation got nervous and began to counter with "all lives matter," as if there were any doubt about that. The hashtag became a movement born of grief, anger, and heartbreak; it has continued to grow, along with demands for accountability from law enforcement, to public officials, to presidential candidates, to the church.

PERSONAL PRAYER

HOW TO PRAY FOR BLACK MEN

Pray as if you are that black boy.
Pray as if you are the bullet.
Pray as if you are tomorrow waiting on him.
Pray as if you are that black boy's mama.
Then pray as if you are that whiteness.
Pray as if you are the witness.
Pray as if you are the curtain through which his killing is witnessed.
Pray as if you are the ground he fell on.
Pray as if you are the blood trying to get away.

Then pray as if you are daylight savings time.
Pray as if you got to break the news to his son.
Pray as if you got to watch the news break.
Pray as if you are the scripture that speaks healing.
Pray as if you can hear black boys crying even when they not.
Then pray as if you know that even God don't know what to say to this.
Pray as if you know people think praying people right up there
    with looters.
Pray as if you are listening for justice.
Pray as if you can't hear none.
Pray as if you black and thinking locked up is safer than jay-walking.
Then pray that no lies about black boys get past you.
Pray as if you are a funeral service.
Pray as if you are the money for a spray.
Pray as if you meet a florist who hates funerals.
Pray as if you know quiet hours can't keep you quiet much longer.
Then pray that the cops don't say that they thought your clasped hands
    was a gun.

COMMUNITY PRAYER*

ONE: People of color die at the hands of police officers (or while in police custody) nearly every day, but some make the news in ways that galvanize the communities and the country. We say their names, honor their memories, pledging to do what we can to stop it, knowing there are so many more:

ALL: **Michael Brown (Ferguson, Missouri) and Sandra Bland (Waller County, Texas). #BlackLivesMatter**

ONE: In New York City, Eric Garner and Shantel Davis. We remember them.

ALL: **Near the nation's capital, Freddie Gray (Baltimore, Maryland) and Miriam Carey (Washington, D.C.). #BlackLivesMatter.**

ONE: Throughout the state of Ohio: Tamir Rice, Tanisha Anderson, Melissa Thomas, and Timothy Russell (Cleveland). John Crawford III (Dayton), and Samuel DuBose (Cincinnati). We remember them.

ALL: Every part of our country is in need of our prayers: Eric Harris (Tulsa, Oklahoma), Rekia Boyd (Chicago, Illinois), Walter Scott (N. Charleston, South Carolina), Jonathan Ferrell (Charlotte, North Carolina), Philado Castile (Falcon Heights, Minnesota), Alton Sterling (Baton Rouge, Louisiana). #BlackLivesMatter

ONE: We can participate in creating a world where peace and justice reign. How will you do your part?

ALL: Do justice, love kindness, and walk humbly with God (Micah 6:8).

There may be reason to add to these lists. We hope there is not one more death, but please adapt this prayer as is needed.

→ • ←

QUESTIONS FOR REFLECTION/ACTION

1. What is one thing you can do to increase understanding and respect and reduce fear and violence?
2. What do you need to learn about someone who is different from you?
3. What would you want someone to know about your experience?

→ • ←

Leslie Carole Taylor serves as the assistant director of Recruitment and Admissions at Pacific School of Religion in Berkeley, California. She graduated from Grinnell College (BA in English), Chicago Theological Seminary (MDiv) and Methodist Theological School in Ohio (DMin). She is an ordained UCC minister and a competitive half-marathon walker.

Marvin K. White is the author of four collections of poetry published by RedBone Press: *Our Name Be Witness, Status* and the two Lambda Literary Award–nominated collections *last rights* and *nothin' ugly fly*. As a community-based artist, he is articulating a vision of social, prophetic, and creative justice through being a black poet, public theologian, artist, teacher, facilitator, activist, community organizer, preacher, homemaker, cake baker, and Facebook "statustician."

20  MERCY INSTEAD OF SACRIFICE
THE EXPENDABILITY OF THE DEATH PENALTY

Suggested Reading: Hosea 6:6, and also see Matthew 12:7

The death penalty is state-sanctioned murder. Capital punishment is based on the misguided belief that the state can determine guilt beyond the shadow of a doubt and that, having done so, should have the right to decide who should live and who should die. It is a perversion of God's justice, the crucifixion of our modern times.

The death penalty is a form of punishment disproportionately applied to people of color and low-income people. It makes social inequality and prejudice into social ills with a fatal end for people in these communities. As the saying goes, those without the capital receive the punishment.

We strip people of their humanity when we put on them the label of "criminal," and then we do away with them, as if any of God's people were expendable. In this way, we avoid examining the structural inequalities that create stratified communities where we don't all have the same access to resources.

When we send people off to death row, we avoid living into the difficult and sacred reality of being God's people in community: we automatically write off the very people Jesus would be likely to both dine and die with. We deny God's glory. We deny God's power. We give up on justice and ignore the fact that many of us live lives without enough: enough resources, enough access to medical care, enough mental health care, enough access to substance abuse treatment, enough education, enough money, enough housing, enough safety, enough love, enough space, enough choices.

Instead of living into God's freedom, we are a society imprisoned by our fear: we would rather put others to death than do the painful and holy work of restoration and healing.

The good news is that we don't have to live this way. We don't have to participate in a culture of fear and punishment. We can live as agents of God's mercy and grace through our activism and advocacy, through our work for justice, through our prayer and our worship, through our connections and our witness. We can be advocates for freedom—for those behind prison walls and for those imprisoned by fear and vengeance as well.

PERSONAL PRAYER

Consider the story of the woman who was fleeing from the crowd that wanted to stone her to death in John 8.

What is it like to experience this story from the point of view of the woman?

What is it like to experience this story from the point of view of the angry crowd with stones in their hands and a law to enforce?

What is it like to experience this story from the point of view of the woman's lover, who is absent from the scene?

Which perspective do you identify most strongly with in your life today?

Are there places in your life that need the challenge that Jesus presents to the crowd?

Are there places in your life that hunger for the freedom he offers?

Spend some time in prayer with the following words, or any of your choosing.

Merciful One,
I hear in myself the echoes of a woman crying in fear and shame.
I feel in myself the weight of those stones of judgment, ready to be cast at the slightest provocation.

Help me to know Christ in me.

Help me to be a reflection of the one who stands for justice, who invites us all into relationship, who offers forgiveness, who embodies grace.

Help me to stand with those whose lives are threatened by judgment.

Help me to stand on the side of mercy.

Help me to daily drop the stones I wish to cast and replace them instead with the gifts of connection, compassion, and community.

In the name of love, I pray.

Amen

COMMUNITY PRAYER

Prayer of Confession

Holy and Merciful One,
free us from fear, we pray.
Free us from turning to human-made, flawed justice
that punishes, isolates, and divides.
Free us from thoughts of revenge and retribution.
Restore us to compassion, O God.

[silent confession]

Assurance of Pardon

Receive today God's pardon, the affirmation and love of community, even as we pray for all those who are awaiting pardons of their own.

Amen

Prayers of the People

We lift up in prayer the names of those who are incarcerated unjustly, those who have been sentenced to death by the state, those who love them and await mercy:

[Add names from your context here]

(If you are in the United States, you can find updated lists of people on death row on the Death Penalty Information Center's website: http://www.deathpenaltyinfo.org/federal-death-row-prisoners.)

Worship Experience—Suggested Reading John 8:7b

We remember the story of the crowd, ready to stone a woman for the sin of adultery, when Jesus offers this radical challenge to look at our own lives before casting the stones that would break this woman's body, break her spirit, and end her life. None of those gathered was able to cast a stone. After they walked away, Jesus said to her, "Woman, where are they? Has no one condemned you?" She said, "No one, sir." And Jesus said, "Neither do I condemn you. Go your way, and from now on do not sin again." John 8:10b–11.

Invite all gathered to pick up a stone to take with them and incorporate it into devotional practice.

Whenever we feel like we are ready to cast judgment or assign blame, we can take up our stone as a reminder.

Whenever we feel like we are superior, without failings, beyond reproach, we can take up our stone in prayer and confession for the ways we inevitably fall short.

Whenever we feel like judgment is falling upon us, we can take up our stone and remember that Jesus has not condemned us, that in Christ we have freedom.

→► • ◄←

QUESTIONS FOR REFLECTION/ACTION

1. If you live somewhere where the death penalty is legal, consider joining local groups working to end the death penalty.

2. Consider writing letters to people who are on death row. Isolation is not God's will for us: let them know that they are not forgotten, that we hold hope and prayer for them and for our broken world.

3. How are your opinions about crime and the legal system, incarceration and capital punishment, really formed and influenced —personal experiences and experiences of family and friends? television and movies? books, blogs, political opinion? ministry

experiences in correctional institutions or faith community discussion? Why might the source of information make a difference?

→>- • -<-

Thea L. Racelis is a Queer Latina minister and theologian. Thea is passionate about God's welcome for all of God's people and Jesus' radical message of social justice and inclusion. She and her spouse, Rikka, live in New England with their small herd of cats.

21 ✳ HUMAN TRAFFICKING
TALITHA KUM,
"LITTLE GIRL, ARISE!"

Few contemporary injustices are as pervasive, as evil, and as damaging to the whole person as human trafficking. In every country, province, city, and neighborhood, humans of all ages, all races, and all backgrounds are being bought and sold. While anybody, regardless of sexual and gender identity, race, ethnicity, age, and socioeconomic background can be trafficked, the vast majority are those marginalized by society—women, transgender persons, children, persons of color, and those living under poverty. These people are more than just victims of a horrendous crime, though—they are beloved children of God, citizens with the saints, and members of the household of God—as St. Paul writes in his letter to the Ephesians.

It is estimated that between twenty-one and thirty million people are bought and sold every year worldwide. Those who are trafficked are drawn into an almost impenetrable cycle of violence, poverty, and abuse by means of force, fraud, and coercion. Human traffickers prey on the most vulnerable in society, those struggling under the bondage of extreme poverty; those oppressed by sexism, homophobia, and transphobia; those who are young and impressionable; those who are lost and lonely. The Christian response to human trafficking must, of course, be to mourn such a grave injustice, but also to pray and to work for change. Ours is a

God of liberation, a God who yearns for freedom, a God who moves from death to life, a God who breaks all chains.

PERSONAL PRAYER

I am weighed down, O God of the living
weighed down with the burden of knowing
that my sisters, my brothers,
your children, your beloved blessed children
are oppressed, enslaved, bought and sold
trafficked on a dark market

I am weighed down, O God of the living
weighed down knowing that
I have contributed to this market
contributed through my actions,
contributed through my inaction

I am weighed down, O God of the living
weighed down with a desire to help,
with a desire to reach out,
to touch, to heal, to free

And you, O God of the living
you are the One who breaks brass doors
the One from whom true freedom flows
the One in whose name all prisoners are set free

Help me, O God of the living
help me set free your daughters, your sons
help me dispel the darkness
help me break the chains

for in you, O God of the living
I find life
I find peace
I find liberation.

COMMUNITY PRAYER

The following can be used in whole (or in part, or altered) for a service of advocacy. It might take place in the congregational setting or outside of the church (for example at a state or federal building or in a park). It is designed to be ecumenical and inclusive, but individuals should feel free to alter language to meet local custom or personal need. Liturgical artists might be creative designing the environment for the liturgy, perhaps even procuring a series of chains and arranging them broken around a cross and/or candle.

Opening Prayer

ONE: Blessed be the God of our salvation

ALL: Who breaks all chains.

ONE: Blessed be the God of our salvation

ALL: Who frees all people.

ONE: Let us pray.

ALL: We come this day, O God, crying out for our sisters and brothers, friends, daughters, mothers, neighbors, beloved who are bought and sold for sex, for labor, or for marriage. Kindle within us a longing for justice and a love for freedom. Bless our praying, our singing, our crying, our advocating, our writing, our healing. Fill us with love, fill us with courage, fill us with hope. We ask this through Jesus the Christ, our brother and friend. Amen

Suggested Reading: Mark 5:35–43

Reflection

It would be ideal for the preacher to be one or several persons who are survivors of human trafficking, whatever the form. If this is not possible or preferable, the speaker might focus reflections on the root causes of human trafficking, paying special attention to the ways that social systems and structures contribute hugely to it. As with any reflection on the gospel, the preacher should end by pointing to the liberty promised in the gospel. "Little girl, get up!" is what Jesus offers to the dead woman. Consider how we, as church, can speak Jesus' words to those who are trafficked.

Prayers of the People

ONE: God weeps with us. God laughs with us. God hears our prayer. For all people bought and sold through human trafficking, we pray.

ALL: O Sun of Justice, hear our prayer.

ONE: For an end to oppressive systems and sinful structures, especially those that prey on those most marginalized, we pray.

ALL: O Sun of Justice, hear our prayer.

ONE: For those who advocate for an end to human trafficking, for those who care forthe trafficked, for those who pray for an end to modern-day slavery, we pray.

ALL: O Sun of Justice, hear our prayer.

ONE: For conversion of heart for those who buy and sell humans, for those who regard humans as commodities, for those ensnared by greed, we pray.

ALL: O Sun of Justice, hear our prayer.

ONE: For those who have died in slavery, for those who have died struggling for freedom, for those who have died alone, we pray.

ALL: O Sun of Justice, hear our prayer.

Closing Prayer

Holy One, the One who breaks chains, the One who sets all free,
you love fiercely the whole human family,
especially those who are enslaved by the sins of society:
the oppressed, marginalized, poor, forgotten, abandoned.
Shine the light of your holy justice
into the darkest corners of our world;
shatter the bonds of slavery, crush the shackles of oppression,
set free those held in bitter captivity;
and fill our hearts and minds
with a fiery passion for justice
so that we can transform

the evil systems and unjust structures
that hold your people hostage.
We ask all of this in the name of Jesus the Liberator.
Amen

→→ • ←←

QUESTIONS FOR REFLECTION/ACTION

1. God desires freedom for all people. What does it mean for privileged people to worship a God who desires liberty for all?

2. Consider the ways in which your personal and shopping habits unknowingly contribute to human trafficking. What habits can you change? What habits can't you change? Why not?

3. There are some groups—women, children, queer people, people of color—who are obviously oppressed. Who else is trafficked and enslaved? What are the root causes of their oppression? How can I/we bring about their liberation?

→→ • ←←

Cody E. Maynus is a student of religious history and frequent commentator on faith and society. He ministers in the Episcopal Church, USA and is discerning monastic life. He currently lives in Minnesota.

We remember Jesus saying that God's realm belongs to little children, and our hearts ache when we hear about children being hurt, neglected, abandoned, or abused. Many of them suffer abuse at the hands of those who should be caring for them. Their youth and vulnerability is taken advantage of and they are forced into silence, afraid and alone.

For every story of abuse that makes it into the twenty-four hour news cycle, countless others go on, unnoted and unresolved. At times, this knowledge can seem, to the outside observer, like an unbearable weight of sadness. We may pray about it at night, or on Sundays. We may ask ourselves and our God why such terrible suffering is inflicted on the most vulnerable population. We may beat our breasts or dig into our bank accounts or search for a way—even a small way—we can help alleviate some of this pain.

All of these things are important, and necessary. We must pray and act with compassion if we want change. We must also remember, though, that many of us are seeing this problem from a place of privilege, a safe haven that those children cannot even imagine. For all the heartache this brings, we must never forget that the pain they feel is greater, and that the need they have for warriors of love is never-ending.

PERSONAL PRAYER

I watch TV
I see the pot bellies of malnourished children,
I see the bruises on abused children,
I see the blank stares of neglected children,
I see the despair of abandoned children,
I watch and I weep.

I read the newspaper
I learn about children who work in factories,
I learn about children who beg in the streets,
I learn about girls who suffer genital mutilation,
I learn about children under unreasonable pressure to succeed in
school,
I learn and I lament.

I look around me
I find children who go to school hungry,
I find children who suffer from preventable diseases,
I find children with no shoes or raincoats,
I find children who are bullied and afraid,
I find things that make me feel guilty.

Loving God,
Stir me to action,
to do what I can for children
in my community,
my country,
and my world.
Give me the courage to speak up for children
to ensure their well-being is considered when decisions are being made.

I would like to gather all children into my loving embrace
but I can't help every child in need.
May there be loving,
giving communities

to care for, value, and protect the children.
In the name of Jesus,
who loved the little children,
I ask these things.
Amen

COMMUNITY PRAYER

Father and Mother of us all
We come before you aware that
sometimes we have failed to love the children in our families
with the love that Jesus showed for them.
We have been impatient with them
rather than slowing down to experience the wonder of your world with
them.
We have tired of their incessant questions
rather than delighting in their curiosity and growing knowledge.
We have squashed their natural exuberance
rather than celebrating it and making space for it.

ALL: **For this we are truly sorry.**

Sometimes we have failed to love the children in our church
with the love that Jesus showed for them.
We have expected them to be silent
rather than valuing their input
We have wanted them to sit still
rather than inviting them to praise God with their bodies
We have prayed and sung using difficult language
rather than speaking simply that all may understand

ALL: **For this we are truly sorry.**

Sometimes we have failed to love the children in our community
with the love that Jesus showed for them.
We have cooed over new babies
rather than helping with the dishes or the washing or the cooking.
We have judged parents for their children's behaviour

rather than lovingly supporting them and relieving their load.
We have ignored the evidence of abuse in our neighbourhood
rather than seeking appropriate help.

ALL: **For this we are truly sorry.**

Sometimes we have failed to love the children in our world
with the love that Jesus showed for them.
We have believed children to be their parents' responsibility
rather than seeing them as our responsibility.
We have ignored government policies that disadvantage children
rather than agitating for change.
We have let children throughout the world suffer
rather than opening our arms and hearts to them as Jesus did.

ALL: **For this we are truly sorry.**

[*A moment's silence*]

ALL: **Holy one,**
Help us to love and value children as Jesus did.
In his name.
Amen

↠ • ↞

QUESTIONS FOR REFLECTION/ACTION

1. What did Jesus mean when he said, "Let the little children come
   to me, and do not stop them; for it is to such as these that the
   kingdom of heaven belongs"? How should this inform our
   worship services?

2. Where do you see children in need in your community? Is there
   an aspect of that need that your church could alleviate?

3. What government policies (local or national) disadvantage children?
   How could these be changed? These are different in different
   countries. I live in Aotearoa/New Zealand. Where do you live?
   What needs to change there?

→→ • ←←

When not wearing her lay preacher's hat and writing liturgy, **Penny Guy** can be found working as a children's librarian in Tauranga, Aotearoa/New Zealand. In this role she reads stories, designs programmes for visiting schools, makes costumes and props, tries out craft activities for holiday programmes, visits schools and preschools, and reads more stories.

23 THE CONTEXT OF CARE
A DANGEROUS ASSUMPTION

The prophet Amos knew that social assumptions could never be sustainable. What God caused him to see was the reality of the injustice and the culture of self-centeredness with all its corruption in his own society. It moved Amos to prayer. From prayer came his compassionate advocacy. It is this that evoked the following insights and "The Amos Prayer: From Lament to Promise" below.

The *assumption of a context of care* for our children as a social norm is betrayed by the terrible statistics of child abuse and murder. New Zealand ranks among the highest in the OECD (Organisation for Economic Co-operation and Development), which includes thirty-five countries, in terms of child abuse and death. What we are faced with is the truth that the norm is quite different from the social assumption. The expression of *an assumption of a context of care* may be expressed as follows: "A parent loves their child so much that they will sacrifice everything for their child."

The contra-indication of that assumption may be expressed in the following: "A parent loves themself so much that they will sacrifice their child for their own life."

And then, in the middle of the thinking, the theory, the protests, there is the silence. Silence filled to the brim with soundless screaming: the unvoiced cry of the voiceless, of the newly born tongue not yet able to form words, of the child who cannot tell, of the vulnerable who can only cry in the heart, *"Who will speak for me?"* This question and its hope is expressed in the following poem of lament and promise formed from the Book of Amos 7:1–6, 9:11–15.

PERSONAL PRAYER

God, our shelter and our home; you care for us in the embrace of your open arms and give us a place at your table; may we who have received so much, in our turn, keep our arms open and a place at our tables of plenty for all your children, so that your healing peace can be known and valued in the lives of all peoples. Amen

THE AMOS PRAYER: FROM LAMENT TO PROMISE

Lament for Jacob
O God, forgive, I beg you!
How can Jacob stand?
He is so small!
He is so small!

O God, I beg you!
How can Jacob call?
His words are not yet formed
He cannot speak at all,
He is so small!

O God, I beg you!
How can this child call?
prisoner of silence
She cannot tell at all
She is so small!

O God, I beg you!
These are your little ones

The least! the vulnerable!
the dying ones!
with voices so small,
or no voice left at all

O God, I beg you!
Hear my call
And let their cries come to you!
or how can I forgive?
forgive you, O God?
O God, of all!

Promise for Jacob
It shall not be
God said to me
That you should forgive
For all you hear
For all you see
Has come from me

It shall not be
that hope is lost!
all the cries,
for justice,
and protesting voices
have surely come to me

they have surely come
See! They have come to you
O my sons O my daughters
sounds of time now come!
hear! the cries of our little ones
now cries of laughter!

though small
they will be strong

their silence will be
the silence of wonder
their voices will be voices
of song

for Jacob will stand!
though he is so small
we will take his
outstretched hand
in ours and hold him,
safe, said God,

you and I, together!

*(Find the Bill Bennett musical setting for this poem at www.napiercathedral
.org.nz under the Worship tab, or at www.youtube.com/watch?v=wtEyiE4bc8U.)*

COMMUNITY PRAYER

Matthew 19:13–15

Matthew tells of the disciples turning away those who brought their children to Jesus. It's as if the children didn't matter. Jesus intervenes and takes time to lay hands on the children. The response of the disciples to those seeking a blessing for their children could be likened to the increasingly punitive welfare structures in which compliance with policy appears to be more important than the well-being of the family.

Luke 8:49–56

By contrast, in the story of the girl restored to life, Luke describes a context of care that does not isolate the family, but in which the community (the disciples), Jesus, and the parents work together for the health of the child. The result is the girl's restoration to life. There is a growing body of evidence suggesting that "wrap-around services" including welfare agencies, family, and community working together provide the best hope of transformation from deprivation to hope.

Candle Lighting Litany

VOICE 1: In sorrow we light this candle
For every child shut in the dark

RESPONSE: **This is my beloved child**

VOICE 2: In sorrow we light this candle
For every child kicked, punched, burned, stomped on

RESPONSE: **This is my beloved child**

VOICE 3: In sorrow we light this candle
For every child whose cries for help go unheard

RESPONSE: **This is my beloved child**

VOICE 4: In sorrow we light this candle
For every child who is killed by a family member, friend, or caregiver

RESPONSE: **This is my beloved child**

VOICE 5: In sorrow we light this candle
For adults who are themselves so damaged they do not know how to care

RESPONSE: **This is my beloved child**

VOICE 1: We light this candle to name
our helplessness in the face of such horror

RESPONSE: **For these are our beloved children**

VOICE 2: We light this candle to name our shame
that so many children live in unsafe families and communities

RESPONSE: **For these are our beloved children**

VOICE 3: We light this candle as a sign of our longing for a society
in which the least and the smallest are cherished and protected

RESPONSE: **For these are our beloved children**

VOICE 4: We light this candle as a sign of our belief
that cycles of intergenerational deprivation can be broken

RESPONSE: **For these are our beloved children**

Voice 5: We light this candle as a sign of our commitment
to the right of every child to safe shelter, loving care,
and welcoming community

Response: **We hold these our children in our hearts and in our prayers.**

↦ • ↤

QUESTIONS FOR REFLECTION/ACTION

1. There are many common signs of child abuse. A few include:
   withdrawal from people or activities; school performance change;
   depression; attempts to run away or hurt oneself; behavior changes,
   which may include defiance, hyperactivity, or aggression toward
   other children; unexplained injuries; sexual knowledge or activity
   beyond age level; frequent headache or stomachache; loss of
   self-confidence. How would you respond if a child you know
   expresses some of these signs? Where would you turn for advice
   on reporting such a symptom?

2. Adults who become abusive or have the potential for abuse are
   God's children. Nearly all of them have been abused or neglected
   themselves. Many are suffering from addiction, financial stress, poor
   understanding of child development, PTSD, or a family crisis such
   as a child with a disability or several children under five years. How
   can faith communities respond with prevention before, or healing
   after, a situation of abuse?

3. Which response to the child abuse crisis makes you most anxious—
   recognition, reporting, rescuing, or rehabilitation?

4. How can you and I move from helplessness to transformative action?

↦ • ↤

Erice Fairbrother is a Benedictine Solitary Oblate of the Order of the Holy Cross in New Zealand. She is a writer, editor, teacher, and published poet. She is particularly committed to promoting poets and poetry as change-making voices for justice and peace.

Erice is part of WILPF (Women's International League for Peace and Freedom) in Napier and of Waiapu Cathedral's Environment Peace and Justice network.

Lynne Frith enjoys playing with words—scrabble, poems, lists, crosswords, prayers—and might one day be brave enough to spray paint words on a wall. When she needs consolation or inspiration she listens to oboe music and sometimes plays the flute or piano. Words and music bring her to life.

24 ✳ SUSTAINABLE RESILIENCE
ABUNDANT LIFE IN
CONNECTION WITH NATURE

Resilient individuals, as well as communities, are capable of accepting difficult situations without losing hope. They are able to believe life has a purpose even in the midst of chaos. The opportunity to spend time in nature strengthens our minds, bodies, and spirits in connection with other people, as well as with the environment. It gives us a chance to develop resilience that is sustainable through the hills and valleys of a lifetime.

Interaction with nature also teaches us about the cycles of life and death, confronts us with suffering, and leads us to recognize the long-term benefits of the processes of change. We learn the rhythms of the seasons and the adaptation of birds, animals, and vegetation to the changes in their environment. We observe, explore, and internalize these experiences into our lives: we, too, can find new life after a tragedy; we too can adapt to the changes around us. Nature is a demanding teacher, but its lessons are not forgotten.

PERSONAL PRAYER

I sit at the feet of beauty.
Once again within
    this friend
    this place
    this time
    this space.

I sit at the feet of beauty.
    Water gushing down the gorge,
    thoughts streaming, one rolling
    after the other, hardly a
    pause until I check the flow. For,

I sit at the feet of beauty.
    I still my mind before
        mountain silhouettes
        river rainbows
        wind whispers
        woodpecker blows.

And listen . . .
    releasing my soul to
        this friend
        this place
        this time
        this space.

COMMUNITY PRAYER

My connection to nature comes from growing up in Mexico City, at that time the second largest city in the world. On evenings when the rain washed away the smog, I delighted in sunsets, watching from the rooftop of our apartment building as the tainted snow turned the Popocateptl and Iztaxihuatl volcanoes pink and orange. I remember my first "on my own" prayer, at age six or so, under a grapefruit tree in the garden, the sun scintillating on fruits and leaves. It was simple. "God, be my friend." To this day, I seek the solace of the outdoors when I need to shift my perspective.

Nature gives us opportunities to learn to *be* with ourselves without the constant noise of external voices, a vital element of resilience, especially as we learn to recognize and tend to our sensations and senses. Nature is the expert teacher of sensations and senses. Our sensations describe how our body feels physically. Are we hot, cold, thirsty, tingly? Why do we feel in a certain way, and what can we do about it?

In the outdoors, we learn to pay attention to and interpret what our body is telling us about ourselves as well as the world around us. These days I am part of the Shalom Center. Nature is still teaching me and others. Consider your context and what its lesson may be as I share mine.

Human senses are those we commonly think of as smell, touch, taste, sight, and hearing, but also include others, such as the following.

Sense of awareness of self, others, and surroundings

The Shalom Center is nestled between a mountain ridge and a river gully in the forest ecosystem of Vilches Alto, Chile. Children and youth from different parts of the country come here to retreat far from electricity and technology. As a boy of ten once stated, "I had such a wonderful time this week, I didn't even miss my best friend." I asked, "What is your best friend's name?" "Television," was his reply. This boy discovered that he was part of a real world beyond the artificial one displayed on a screen.

Sense of solitude

In preparation for a solo walk through a forest that is both thriving and recovering from charcoal production, I share my experience with the children. "When I walk alone on the path and I see the destroyed parts of the forest, I think about awful things have that happened to me. I feel hope when I see new trees growing. I let go of my pain by imagining that I throw it over the edge of the cliff into the river below. Then, I am ready to be with people again."

Sense of wonder and curiosity

One of my favorite photos from my work is of a city school teacher on knees and elbows in a tight circle of similarly positioned children, eyes and mouths open in amazement, watching a four-inch-long beetle laying eggs in a hole in the ground. Whenever we meet, the teacher and the children remind me excitedly about the experience.

Sense of timing

At the Shalom Center, children and adults form a community where the sense of timing uplifts and embraces each person's dignity and needs. Forest timing, cool time and heat, light and dark, rain and sunshine—it all teaches us that there is a time to laugh and sing, a time to be quiet and listen, a time to pray and think, a time to eat and sleep, a time to run and shout with glee.

Sense of connection

A researcher monitoring deep water wells in northern California recently told me that when the earthquake struck Chile on February 27, 2010, just after 3:30 AM, his team knew something terrible had happened somewhere in the world. They saw the waves in the groundwater sensors. The rumbling I heard that night deep underground at the Shalom Center traveled thousands of miles and disturbed the ground water in northern California. Tree roots and mountains stretch far down into the earth and extend through gravel, water, and even continental plates to groundwater, mountains, and trees on the other side of the world. I invite the children, when sitting under "Mother Hen," the ancient coigue tree at the Shalom Center, to imagine that they are connected through her roots to any other part of the world. We are intertwined with all life on our amazing planet!

→ • ←

QUESTIONS FOR REFLECTION/ACTION

1. I often have compared myself to a tenacious dandelion growing in the crack of a cement sidewalk. What plant or animal would you compare yourself to and why?

2. Take a moment to remember a few of your favorite childhood memories when you felt happy, peaceful, and carefree. How many of these memories are associated in some way with nature or the outdoors? How are these memories part of your resilience?

3. What are the gifts that nature might have waiting for you in the place where you live—country or city? What outdoor activities could help you develop an awareness of yourself and the needs of the wider community and earth?

→→ • ←←

"The world, our classroom; nature, our teacher." As a missionary with Global Ministries of the Christian Church (Disciples of Christ) and the United Church of Christ, **Elena Huegel** uses a variety of imaginative methods to create a context for cultivating dignity, resilience, and healing.

25 · SAFE SPACES
HEALING FROM CHILDHOOD SEXUAL ABUSE

Despite the work of various advocacy groups and increased public awareness, childhood sexual abuse is still an ongoing tragedy in the United States. Some statistics report one in five girls and one in ten boys have been victimized, often by a family member or someone they believed they could trust. Without help, the effects of this betrayal may cause long-lasting symptoms such as depression or self-harm, or lead to addiction or posttraumatic stress as adults. It should be no surprise, given the statistics, that there are victims and survivors in our congregations. Thankfully, most religious organizations now have guidelines in place to help their congregations create safer spaces.

In my work with children and youth, I provide training for teachers and volunteers. Every volunteer fills out a background release form, which is kept on file. Using a form of appreciative inquiry, we share stories about times we've felt safe. We list the things that made us feel safe and, as a consequence, discover the underlying values we hold about safe spaces for ourselves and the children and youth in our care. In addition, we try to help children and youth keep strong personal boundaries.

PERSONAL PRAYER

Suggested Reading: Isaiah 43:18–19

She could not remember what startled her,
what she saw out of the corner of her eye.
When she turned to look, it was gone.

She woke up unable to breathe,
"Who is it?" she cried, not knowing why.

Over time she found nothing
to keep the truth hidden—
Not food, alcohol, lovers, shopping—
nothing as powerful as the truth

I am thinking of getting help, she said tentatively.

I ENCOURAGE you to do it!
a long-listening friend replied.

So she took the first steps on the healing path
She began to remember the past
so terrifying she thought it would kill her

"Will there ever be a day, an hour
I don't spend remembering?"

Yes, a friend from the other side
of terror assured her.
So she held onto those words until they were true.

*In my work with youth, I have had the opportunity to collect a number of prayers,
made anonymous to protect the identities of those who wrote them. Here are a
couple of them.*

Noire

*In preparation for Youth Sunday at our church, the youth spent the weekend mak-
ing and painting plaster cast masks.*

"Under this mask is a deep dark secret *no one* will ever know," she shouted, then sobbed to keep from saying more. Later she told me, with a promise not to tell. She was eighteen and she was safe now. Except, of course, for the secret keeping her from love or ever feeling free.

Noire's Prayer

God, you know how I pushed away all of my memories, both good and bad, to survive the dark times. You remember how scared and angry I was every day. I felt so different because I didn't understand what was happening to me. Thank you for giving me friends who took me to a church where I found my way out of the darkness. They let me be angry. They were patient when I obsessed over video games, and they respected the fact I did not like to be touched. Help me continue my journey through and hold me in the light. Please be with other kids who are going through what I went through. Amen

Sam

"My mother died," he said, "and my stepfather sexually abused me. I hate him. That's why I'm changing my name from the one he gave me. I've been in foster care for years. They beat me with a belt and sometimes I wanted to die. Now I have a family, a real family—two dads who don't hurt or give up their children."

Sam's dads dedicate themselves to helping Sam and their other two sons develop confidence and become successful. This has meant countless counseling appointments and evenings of homework help as well as an endless flow of teens and young adults in their home.

Dad's Prayer

God, please fill my heart with abundant love for my new family. Give me the words to say when things get tough. Give me courage not to give up and strength to push ahead. Help me to comfort them when they cry. Let me know when to hold them and let me know when to let them be alone to deal with their past. Help me sense when to spend more time thinking about the future. And, most importantly, help me to not be hurt when they talk about their "real" mom or dad. I am where I am supposed to be and the kids who live with me and their friends, who have also become a part of my family, have given me a house and heart filled with laughter and love. Sure, there are bad times, but all families have good and bad. Since my kids have had too many bad times, we concentrate on creating good times and trying to let our kids know nothing is wrong with them and they are going to have great lives filled with so much love. Thank you. Amen

COMMUNITY PRAYER

Lover of children, you call us to approach life with the wonder and delight of a child. We thank you for the children you have placed in our life. There are children who are suffering abuse at the hands of someone using their power and influence to silence them. Do not abandon them to their tormentors, O God.

Holy One, show us a way to be a part of the healing path for children who are being sexually abused by people they should be able to trust. We know there are adults who still carry the secret of having been sexually abused as children, who still cannot be free from their past. Give us a willingness to hear all the hard stories of abuse, O God, and equip us with the gift of encouragement to help victims find hope and healing and advocacy to change the world for children in the future. Amen

→ • ←

QUESTIONS FOR REFLECTION/ACTION

1. Imagine the children you love. How do they delight you? What ways do they show you beauty in the world? Surround them with your love and give thanks for them.

2. Imagine the terror of children who might be enduring abuse this day. Surround these unknown children with your love.

3. Are there ways you can consider becoming a safe person in the life of such a child or adult? Open your heart to this possibility. Consider taking a workshop or a reading a book on the topic.

Lucy Brady has been called to be an advocate and an activist in the United States for those who are victims of childhood sexual abuse. In her previous urban congregation, and in her present small town congregation, many disclosed their stories of abuse. As a result, some people went to jail, some received help, and, in the midst of helping others, a past long buried began to emerge. Today, she is not defined by the trauma of that past, and she continues to support others whose past keeps them from living a full life.

26 ✳ TEACHING CONSENT
EMPOWERING CHOICE
FOR ALL PEOPLE

One of my favorite things to do with children is schedule our time together in stations. Instead of deciding on my own how to dictate our activities, I set up three or four options for them. For example, at Earth Day one year, they could choose between making art from trash, snack creation, or writing practice. When one boy decided he didn't want to do any of the stations, I had to make a choice. I could insist that he join one of the tables—didn't he know I'd chosen good options for him? Or I could remind him that he needed to spend time doing something constructive, something that would help him grow. He looked at me and said, "Well, can I read?"

The children I work with have very few options in their lives. In the best circumstances, they have three meals a day and clothes to wear and a story to read and school to go to. But they don't get to choose any of those things. A parent or guardian decides what the best meal would be or what clothes will suit them or what book to read or whether/when/ how it's time to go to school.

As adults, we assume we are making the best choices for the children in our lives. We may even believe it's best to make those choices because we know better, and sometimes we do.

We know, for example, that it really is better to stay out of the street, or that carrots are healthier than cupcakes. It's wise to put on a coat when it's snowing and to keep our fingers out of electrical sockets. But we do not need to make every choice for a child, and we shouldn't make every decision without a child's input. We must build a child's capacity for consent and for the sense that her choices are valid.

Whenever we make a choice for a child without asking his opinion, we play into a narrative that this person has opinions that do not matter, that his feelings and experience don't count. Part of making choices is the ability to say no and to have that "no" be heard. Someday, that child may be faced with harder choices or with no choice at all. One in three women will be sexually assaulted in their lifetime, and one in four men will be. The choice made for them—to them—is not something they should have to live with, nor is the feeling that another person has power over their bodies or their basic human rights. "No" is always a valid choice and "no" should always be enough.

When we welcome children into the decision making, when we teach them that their opinion and consent matters, we develop a child's ability to know her own heart and mind and that "no" is a powerful and accessible answer.

PERSONAL PRAYER

Dear God,

Help me to know when to offer choices so I can empower the children in my life to learn the boundaries of consent and respect. There are too many people in this world who have the right to say no taken from them, and I want to be a person who listens and who fights for "no" to mean "no." Help me to use any privilege and power I may have to listen and support all those who feel silenced and powerless. Help my heart to be moved, and move my feet to action.

In the name of the one who hears the voiceless and heals the broken, I pray. Amen

COMMUNITY PRAYER

The community gathers together in a circle with children at the center. The community members should self-select into adults, children, and youth. If the children are young for liturgical reading invite them to make pictures in advance of either a smiling face (happy minds) or a decorated heart (big heart). Each one should choose which design to create.

ADULTS: God, we pray for open ears and open hearts. We who are grown think we have all the answers. Help us live with wisdom and teach with love.

YOUTH: God, we pray for open minds and open hearts. We who are still discovering ourselves will hurt and worry and think we have all the answers. Help us live with curiosity and learn with grace.

CHILDREN: God, we pray for happy minds and big hearts. We want to grow and learn. Help us speak up and help us listen. *Children should show their pictures. An older child can read this line in short segments for an echo effect.*

ADULTS: We look to you, the young ones in our community. Help us live so that you trust us. Help us listen to you.

YOUTH: We look to you, the older ones in our community. Help us listen to you and help us trust our own decisions. Empower us. We look to you, children, knowing that we still have to grow.

CHILDREN: We look to you, our (church/school) family. Help us grow and help us learn. Let us choose what we can. Teach us "yes." Teach us "no." Teach everyone "listen."

ALL: Let us love each other. Amen

⤜ ● ⤛

QUESTIONS FOR REFLECTION/ACTION

1. When and where have you felt the most empowered to say no or to say yes? When and where have you felt the least empowered?

2. Write or draw about a time you felt you had no choices. Did you get your voice back? How? If not, how has that affected your ability both to make choices and to offer them to others?

3. What boundaries and limits are there in giving a child a choice? Does it matter by age/gender/place? Why?

4. After thinking about the importance of choice and consent in children's lives, are there parallels with others who often have decision making taken away from them—such as frail elders, elders with some dementia, people with developmental disabilities, people with limited English language skills, people burdened by poverty or lack of education? How can our reflections here be applied to others?

→‑ • ‑←

abby mohaupt is a Presbyterian Church (USA) pastor, long distance runner, crayon artist, partner to Nathan, and caregiver to two sweet felines. She has a Master's of Divinity and Master's of Theology from McCormick Theological Seminary. She is currently working on a PhD in Religion and Society at Drew University.

THE WEEPING WOMB

27 ✳ LIFE'S LIMITATIONS WITH FEMALE REPRODUCTIVE HEALTH ISSUES

Women and girls across the world face reproductive health issues—polycystic ovarian syndrome (PCOS), endometriosis, fibroid tumors, and reproductive cancers, among other ailments. These conditions can result in debilitating chronic pain, infertility, or intimacy issues as well as loss of productivity and time with loved ones. Furthermore, in the process of dealing with these illnesses, sufferers often must incorporate multiple doctor appointments, tests, and treatments into their lives. Time and monetary resources can be exhausted. In many countries around our world, resources are not readily available. Finally, there can be shame that accompanies disease symptoms and medication side effects, and it brings additional burdens and heartaches to the many who suffer.

PERSONAL PRAYER

Mother God, the wombs of women and girls of all ages cry out to you in horrific pain, shame, discouragement, and sadness. Options for cures are few. The anguish rages on.

Like fire burning within our bodies, we wonder what's next for us. *What pain level will I experience tomorrow? What new symptom will appear? Will I be able to afford medications? Will I relapse?*

And yet, our bodies carry on even when our uteruses are broken. When the waves of agony crash upon us, we still faithfully work, serve you, and care for family and friends.

Sometimes, we question whether you exist in the stillness of our sadness. *Are you bringing us peace as we curl on beds in a fetal position? Are you comforting us when the tears spring forth from our souls? Are you strengthening us when guilt overcomes our lives?*

And so we wait.

Even through the film of frustration and discouragement, we see healing on the horizon. No amount of anguish will stop us from praying for new methods of healing. We think of our sisters across our world where medical help is sparse or expensive, and eradicating the disease is an unattainable dream. We look to your presence to comfort us as we wait with patience for solutions.

Even when our capacity for hope shrinks year after year, the seeds of possibility remain in the cold, dormant ground. As research is completed, as more speak of their experiences with these illnesses, and as new medications become available, we give thanks. The ground is warming. Our frozen anticipation thaws.

May we work together to shed illness, infertility, indignity, and isolation from the lives of women and girls across the world and to educate those who have no context or understanding of our concerns, knowing that anything is possible through your call, Mother God. Amen

COMMUNITY PRAYER

Litany for the Blessing of Wombs

The nameless woman with the hemorrhage from Mark 5 reflects many of our lives and the lives of our loved ones. She is smiling through her pain, working through her weakened state, caring through the roller coaster of hormones, and showing her face in the midst of shame. And so we pray for her today.

Suggested Reading: Mark 5:25–34

ONE: We lift the ones whose never-ending intense pain extends across their pelvis and stabs their back.

MANY: **May the hem of Christ relieve them.**

ONE: We pray for our sisters whose illness leads to symptoms that cause embarrassment, including excess hair growth, weight fluctuation, infertility, and incontinence.

MANY: **May the hem of Christ erase their shame.**

ONE: We pray for the women whose treatments cause side effects of nausea, depression, anxiety, hot flashes, and additional pain.

MANY: **May the hem of Christ give them strength to endure.**

ONE: We pray for the ones whose discomfort keeps them immobile and whose static lives usher in discouragement.

MANY: **May the hem of Christ give them patience in their healing.**

ONE: We lift the ones whose wombs are closed, where scar tissue and adhesions have sealed the uterus and fallopian tubes. We pray that any desire for fertility and parenthood will be fulfilled.

MANY: **May the hem of Christ erase the tangles of despair.**

ONE: We pray for the girls who were born without a uterus or with ill-functioning ovaries.

MANY: **May the hem of Christ fill them with contentment as they grow.**

ONE: We pray for the women who experience miscarriage, the emptying of the energy-filled womb. May hope blossom within them once again.

MANY: **May the hem of Christ bring them peace in the depths of loss.**

ONE: We pray for ones whose bodies prohibit them from enjoying intimacy due to pelvic pain. We pray for the spouses and partners who care for their loved ones, even when intimate acts aren't possible without pain.

MANY: **May the hem of Christ heal them, and may the hem of Christ bind these couples together.**

ONE: We pray for our transgender brothers who must endure health challenges with their remaining reproductive organs and our transgender sisters who live without a desired uterus. May they find the peace and harmony among their body, mind, heart, and soul.

MANY: **May the hem of Christ give them comfort.**

ONE: We pray that systems will open and medications deemed optional or controversial will become affordable to those with these health issues.

MANY: **May the hem of Christ be within their reach.**

ONE: We pray for the voices who have come forward to speak about their struggles and whose words bring others hope and solidarity.

MANY: **May the hem of Christ bring them courage.**

ONE: We pray for the days when the news seems less than hopeful, when fertility seems distant and discomfort seems close at hand. As the never-ending anguish thrives within our hearts—

MANY: **May the hem of Christ usher in the harmony of our bodies, minds, and souls.**

Each person with a personal struggle or intercession for a loved one will come to a healing station to receive a blessing (or lift their hand and someone will come to them). If the recipient would like, they can receive a blessing on their lower abdomens. Anoint their wombs by placing the sign of the cross immediately below their navel. For all other persons receiving the blessing, place the sign of the cross on their foreheads.

⇥ • ⇤

QUESTIONS FOR REFLECTION/ACTION

1. How do people in different contexts face these issues? For instance, how might the experiences of a teenage girl with endometriosis differ from those of a woman in her early forties? How would the experience of a woman with PCOS in the United States or United Kingdom be different from that of a woman in India, Ghana, or Tonga?

2. In what ways do we have compassion or lack consideration for our friends who must cancel or change plans because of their reproductive health issues?

3. What legislation has passed in our country recently, and where are there gaps in legislation to ensure girls and women have the health care they need?

⇥ • ⇤

Michelle L. Torigian is the pastor of St. Paul United Church of Christ, Old Blue Rock, in Cincinnati, Ohio. A 2010 graduate of Eden Theological Seminary, Torigian has had essays in the books *There's a Woman in the Pulpit* (Skylight Paths Publishing) and *Sacred Habits: The Rise of the Creative Clergy* (Noesis Press). Her writings can be found at the Huffington Post Religion page, RevGalBlogPals, the UCC's New Sacred, and her own blog, michelletorigian.com.

28 EXTREME VIOLENCE AGAINST ABORIGINAL WOMEN AND GIRLS IN CANADA PRAYERS FOR THOSE WHO DIE, PRAYERS FOR THOSE WHO GRIEVE, PRAYERS FOR THOSE WHO KILL

Approximately twelve hundred women and girls identified as "Indigenous" have been murdered in Canada in the past twenty years—a homicide rate several times higher than that of all other Canadian women. In addition, one out of every three native women endures sexual assault in her lifetime. This violence is the result of the combined legacy of racism, misogyny, marginalization, and poverty leaving Indigenous women vulnerable to extreme violence, kidnapping, and, in far too many cases, murder. These horrific crimes are epidemic, yet largely ignored. The voices of the victims are silenced, their stories untold.

PERSONAL PRAYER

We pray for those who have died.

Spirit of Holy Places,
Into your hands we entrust our sisters. Taken from this world in violence, may they journey to the next world in peace. In this life you embraced

our sisters with your steadfast love; deliver them now from every evil and call them into eternal rest.

We pray for those who grieve.

Redeemer of the Sorrowful,
Our brother Jesus wept at the death of Lazarus and assured his followers that those who mourn shall be comforted. We long for your presence in every loss. Grant us your peace.

We pray for those who kill.

God of Forgiveness and Redemption,
Jesus uttered the words: *forgive them for they know not what they do,* because the suffering was his to forgive. We ask now that God hold those we can forgive and those for whom the forgiveness is not ours to offer.
In the whispering breath of the Spirit,
In the persistent redemption of the Christ,
In the eternal love of the God of all peoples, we say *amen.*

COMMUNITY PRAYER

A Call to Worship Adapted from Psalm 102

Do not hide your face from me in the day of my distress. Incline your ear to me; answer me speedily in the day when I call. For my days pass away like smoke, and my bones burn like a furnace.

RESPONSE: **Hear my prayer, O God; let my cry come to you.**

I am like a solitary bird on a lonely branch, my days like an evening shadow; I wither away as grass drying in the desert sun. I travel a highway of tears and never come to rest.

RESPONSE: **Hear my prayer, O God; let my cry come to you.**

But you, O Lord, are enthroned forever; your name endures to all generations. You will rise up and have compassion on our sisters, for it is time to rescue all those who suffer at the hands of aggressors; the appointed time has surely come.

RESPONSE: Hear my prayer, O God; let my cry come to you.

The powerful will fear the name of God. For God will build up the people, appearing in glory. God will regard the prayers of the destitute, and will not be oblivious to their pleas.

RESPONSE: Hear my prayer, O God; let my cry come to you.

God has looked down from the Holy Mountain to hear the groans of the prisoners, to set free those doomed to die. When every woman is safe, then will the name of God be declared in all the earth.

RESPONSE: Amen

→→ • ←←

QUESTIONS FOR REFLECTION/ACTION

1. Who does not know about the terrible endangerment of Aboriginal women in Canada? Who does not know the depths of grief of those who mourn? Now that you know, how can you share this story?

2. Imagine offering forgiveness to a person who physically harmed or even killed someone you love. What does that forgiveness feel like? Does Jesus' commandment to love one another have limits for you? Describe any boundaries that you imagine.

→→ • ←←

Before becoming an ordained minister in the United Church of Christ, **Jane A. Willan** worked as a science editor, a freelance writer, a researcher, and a teacher. She loves reading, camping, and hiking with her dogs and husband. She spends her free time writing cozy mystery novels (as yet unpublished).

INDIAN RESIDENTIAL
SCHOOLS IN CANADA
FACING A HORRIBLE TRUTH

There are three words in the English lexicon that are more powerful than any conventional weapon. They have consistently been used by imperialist regimes around the globe in India and Africa, Australia and New Zealand, the United States and Canada. The spell-casting phrase is: "I Know Better"!

Girded with the certitude that "I know better," Sir John A. Macdonald appointed himself Canadian Minister of Indian Affairs and inaugurated the policy of withholding food from Aboriginal people until they were coerced onto reserves as the Canadian Pacific Railway made its way across the country. Subsequently he boasted that the Aboriginal population was kept on the "verge of actual starvation to deflect criticism that I was squandering public funds."

MacDonald was even more confident when he launched the residential school system to "take the Indian out of the child." In the young ambitious Duncan Campbell Scott, the prime minister found a willing acolyte who would outlive him and continue this cultural genocide for decades. The personal certainty "I know better" allowed Scott to maintain a duplicitous attitude. In his official capacity he advocated: "'The happiest future for the Indian race is absorption into the general population, and this is the object and policy of our government—Assimilation!" Yet, this same man, as an admired poet, dissembled his true intentions in evocative words idolizing Aboriginal people.

Recently churches and governments have offered apologies renouncing past attitudes, carefully embroidered in reconciliation rhetoric. Still, policies remain laden with paternalism, implying that Aboriginal people have not yet earned equality of opportunity, nor are they capable of properly administering their own affairs. Although the notion that "I know better" may have morphed in application, the dominant society appears to remain determinedly subscribed in principle. God grant that one day every Canadian will realize that we are all "Treaty People"!

PERSONAL PRAYER

Gizhe-manidoowiwin, Divine Nature, we reflect upon the deplorable legacy of Indian Residential Schools in Canada. This blight was inflicted upon our people for one hundred and twenty-five years, and only on the Millennia was the last federally operated school closed. And so we lift up:

- ♦ the roughly one hundred fifty thousand children compelled to attend the residential schools;

- ♦ the four thousand who died attending a residential school and their lonely, unmarked, lost graves;

- ♦ the thousands of parents who grieved their children being abducted and removed to school;

- ♦ the hundreds of thousands of grandparents denied their proper role of sharing culture, language, and spirituality with their grandchildren;

- ♦ the communities that withered and died without a younger generation to reinvigorate;

- ♦ the thousands of children exposed to serious illnesses in deplorable conditions;

- ♦ the roughly seventy-eight thousand former students who survived the system, but still carry physical, emotional, and spiritual scars;

- the thousands of residential school survivors condemned to dependancy, addiction, and chronic illness;
- the children and grandchildren of residential school students suffering from the syndrome of multigenerational abuse;
- those misguided European settlers who assumed their civilization was the pinnacle of human achievement and genuinely believed that they knew best;
- teachers, clergy, support staff, police officers, bureaucrats, agents, and others compelled to function in a system they didn't support, and who were themselves victimized by the process.

And we celebrate the generations who exposed abuses perpetrated upon them and brought this system to an overdue end at last;

and those who gather and reconstitute the disparate elements of culture, language, and spirituality scattered and destroyed by the residential school system;

Finally, Creator, we ask a blessing upon all who in their everyday lives quietly demonstrate an attitude of reconciliation and egalitarianism, so that such travesties as the residential school system never happen again. Amen

COMMUNITY PRAYER*

I am a white woman. Five generations ago my ancestors came from England to this land called Canada. They had never owned land before. The promise of free land was like a dream, and so they came. They came in rickety ships, through ice and storm, by cart and by foot to a rocky, desolate, windswept place. A place where they planted and toiled and lived a life harder then they could have imagined. They were devout and honest people. Hardworking people. They did not know, nor did their children, nor their children's children know, the horrible price paid for that life and that land.

That knowledge has fallen to me.

It is a horrible truth.

Seven generations of human beings—the First Peoples of Canada—were, and continue to be, cheated, robbed, beaten, incarcerated, starved, infected, poisoned, murdered, abused, stolen, misrepresented, unrepresented, ignored, and almost-but-not-quite annihilated for land. For the land I call home and the life I call mine.

The Truth and Reconciliation Commission of Canada has brought public attention to the truths of colonialism and residential schools and their multigenerational impact on Indigenous peoples and Canada as a whole. It also offered real, practical solutions that begin with building relationships with each other—getting to know each other.

My ancestors were not bad people. They were ordinary people caught up in an evil system. Gandhi once wrote; "You assist an evil system most effectively by obeying its orders and decrees. An evil system does not deserve such allegiance." Breaking allegiance with an evil system begins with lament, followed by repentance. Redemption is promised, and justice flows forth like a healing stream.

Litany of Lament

LEADER: If you are prepared to lament your complicity in an evil system, then say these words. If you are not ready, remain silent, holding them in your heart until they can stay there no longer.

Join together in reciting Psalm 32:3–5.

ALL: While I kept silence, my body wasted away
through my groaning all day long.
For day and night your hand was heavy upon me;
my strength was dried up as by the heat of summer. Selah
Then I acknowledged my sin to you,
and I did not hide my iniquity;
I said, "I will confess my transgressions to God,"
and you forgave the guilt of my sin. *Selah*

LEADER: Hearts have been broken.

GATHERED: I lament that I have knowingly, and unknowingly, broken hearts.

LEADER: Bodies have been broken

GATHERED: I lament that I have knowingly, and unknowingly, broken bodies.

LEADER: Spirits have been broken.

GATHERED: I lament that I have knowingly, and unknowingly, broken spirits.

LEADER: Our connection with the land and with each other has been broken.

GATHERED: My heart cries out . . . Holy One, come to our hearts, our bodies, our spirits, and bring healing.

Prayer of Repentance

LEADER: Holy God, we confess that we have been complicit in an evil system.

GATHERED: Our complicity has allowed those in power to turn a blind eye to injustice and ignore the pleas of the suffering. Our complicity has harmed fellow human beings.

LEADER: Holy God, we confess that we have served an evil system.

GATHERED: With our eyes to the grindstone and our heads in dreams of self-gratification, we have not seen the plight of others. We have been blinded by lies and allowed ourselves the believe delusions fed to us by a system that seeks to keep us distracted and silent.

LEADER: Holy God, we repent and turn ourselves to you.

GATHERED: Take us, O God, as we are, and receive our humble willingness to be transformed by the horrible truths we face into the people you would have us be.

LEADER: We hear the words of the psalmist who wrote in Psalm 32:8–11:
I will instruct you and teach you the way you should go;
I will counsel you with my eye upon you.

Do not be like a horse or a mule, without understanding,
whose temper must be curbed with bit and bridle,
else it will not stay near you.
Many are the torments of the wicked,
but steadfast love surrounds those who trust in God.
Be glad in God and rejoice, O righteous,
and shout for joy, all you upright in heart.

ALL: In you, O God, we trust. In you, O God, we rejoice. Amen

*In the final words of the litany in "Community Prayer" Patti Rodgers paraphrased segments from "A Song of Faith, A Statement of Faith of the United Church of Canada, l'Église Unie du Canada," www.united-church.ca/community-faith /welcome-united-church-canada/song-faith.

→ • ←

QUESTIONS FOR REFLECTION/ACTION

1. What do you know about apologies? Four Anglo settler countries—New Zealand, Australia, Canada, and the United States, and provinces/states within them—have apologized to Indigenous peoples. Religious communities, from missionary denominations in Hawai'i to Pope Francis in Bolivia, have also done so. Some of these have been the result of intentional processes and others legislative votes. Learn something about historical apologies.

2. The Blanket Exercise is a small group activity of KAIROS: Canadian Ecumenical Justice Initiatives that attempts to replace fictionalized history often taught in school with the truth of the Indigenous reality. Its intent is not to elicit guilt, but often a sense of personal culpability is the reaction of dominant society participants. It's not uncommon for people to voice apologies for the abuse perpetrated against Indigenous peoples—instances they weren't even aware of a couple of hours earlier.

3. Consider . . . some people resent or avoid making an apology on
   behalf of historical injustice . . . some people escape reparations or
   support through apology . . . some people have their lives transformed through apology. How do you feel about apology?

4. "We will raise your children." The Canadian residential schools
   are one example of a dominant society ripping children from their
   culture and attempting to fill them with another one. This crime
   has been repeated many places. An urban elementary teacher in the
   United States this week told me that her African American students
   suffered environmental failure because most of the examples on a
   standardized test were rural. What are contemporary examples of
   "educating" children away from their cultures?

↦ • ↤

Patti Rodgers is a lay minister serving a two-point pastoral charge just north of Toronto, Canada. Before officially becoming a "minister," she ministered by providing adminis-trative support to the Aboriginal Ministries Circle of the United Church of Canada, and as one of a team of family law professionals. She is a mother and grandmother.

R. Matthew Stevens: Being a person of Métis heritage (sometime referred to as "mixed blood") I consider myself particularly fortunate to be able to occupy a space between cultures, with access to both. I've been privileged to learn many of the traditional teach-ings from some very gifted and patient Elders, and to have availed myself of some excellent formal education as well. From both of these sources I have learned how disabling a pervasive sense of guilt can be to an individual, and how collectively it can incapacitate society from appropriately redressing prevailing circumstances.

30  SILENCED HISTORIES
REDISCOVERY, CELEBRATION, AND MOURNING

Jesus paid attention to people that the culture ignored; he listened to those society silenced; he included those the powerful rejected; he extended compassion to those the empire viewed as the least, the last, the lost.

As Christ followers, we are called to ask, Who are the people in our neighborhood, in our area, in our world who are invisible, silenced, rejected, valued least? Whose stories, perspectives, values, or histories are marginalized and even erased?

Consider indigenous people, those of African descent, the economically marginalized, or those who do not speak the dominant language, to name a few. How might rediscovering and celebrating silenced history stretch the circle of compassion, widen the welcome table, and fire the passions of justice? Walking in the way of Jesus calls us to this challenge.

PERSONAL PRAYER

Can anything good come from Nazareth, they ask.

Yet, the Way, the Truth, and the Life manifests itself in the Great Story, in the life of Jesus that models faithfulness in the midst of empire. This Way intentionally includes the invisible, the marginalized, and the silenced.

Interrupt our habitual consumption of media, Holy One. Break through our usual echo-chambers. Stir in us new questions about underlying assumptions, perspectives, and purpose. Lead us to become curious about how our personal allegiances shape our newsfeeds. Open our eyes and ears to the fear-infused reporting, the excluded voices, the untold histories, the cries in Ramah, the censorship in service of the powerful.

In the midst of information overload, teach us to ground ourselves in you. May the Holy Spirit guide our selection of media stories, and reveal your good news in this time and place.

In Jesus' name we pray. Amen

COMMUNITY PRAYER

Twelve Years a Child

Summer school begins in twelve days. It's been twelve days since the Fourth of July—a day to remember the price paid for our freedom—"one nation, under God, indivisible, with liberty and justice for all." Today is also Devon's twelfth birthday.

His only gift, a cap gun, is three miles away, stored in his best friend's home. When he arrives, Devon recognizes Manny even at a distance. They wear identical white baseball caps, a gift they received three years ago at a local church's Youth & Police event. The initials on the white caps, B.N.A. (Be Not Afraid), remind both of them *God is with us*. Devon has plans though, and he's in a hurry to get to the gazebo before dark. Gripping his toy gun and stuffing the cap gun papers in his pockets, Devon thanks Manny and takes off down the road.

Despite heavy traffic and bike-eating potholes, he arrives at the empty park and leans against the gazebo; finally he's alone in his favorite place, a shelter from the storms in his life. Here, he can explore his new toy out from under his mother's watchful eye. Here, he can play with the gift he had hoped to get for Christmas but had to wait six more months to receive. He imagines his mother's voice. "No guns for Christmas! *Child*, have you lost your mind?"

Devon is immersed in his new toy. He notices a broken yellow safety cap on the tip of the gun's nose. That doesn't matter, he thought. The gun's trigger works, and the loud popping sounds are reminiscent of the Fourth of July fireworks. He doesn't even see the squad car pull up—doesn't notice the men in uniform stop their patrol car in front of him. He hears the siren blip, just once, and looks up, startled. Is there trouble?

After that, everything happens so fast. He hears a sound much louder than a toy cap gun. One second, two seconds, Devon falls, stretched out on the ground and fighting for his life. Three, four, five seconds, the perpetrator dressed as a protector pours bullets into him. The sound of the real gun is a hundred times louder than his toy.

Less than a minute to go from bright, curious, celebrating child to young brown body in a pool of blood. Violence replaces the joy of the park, the serenity of the gazebo. Passersby watch Devon's life slip away—a cloud of witnesses as the scene unfolds.

When his family arrives, the cries of his sister and mother are enough to raise the dead. But no one calls out, "Wake up, Lazarus!"

Lament

Nobody prayed for Devon, man-child, little boy, and twelve-year-old soul.
Nobody heard anybody pray for somebody's boy.
For somebody's son, anybody's baby brother, a boy's best friend. Nobody prayed again, no one prayed for him!
Darkness covered the gazebo.

Two mothers hold each other and invite others to pray:
Lord, have mercy,
For brown babies, brown boys, and their friends.
Why are some destined to be boys and never men?
Their presence is obvious yet innocence never seen.

Two fathers embrace like branches on trees,
They park and pray on bended knees,
"Please, come, park, and pray for us with me,
Let's pray, Lord, hear our prayer, Lord, listen, please.
Lord of sight, Lord of sound, Lord of power and Light,
Shine on us, raise and turn stubborn hearts around."

We pray for strangers, who study shades of brown,
Brown boys and brown men, whose innocence never found,
We pray for the strangers, who tremble,
Strangers who act strange,
Strange strangers who fear brown boys, brown men who come near.
We pray, Lord, have mercy on brown, black, white boys and men.

Have mercy Oh God, on all who fear them,
Our allies pray, God have mercy on brown babies,
Pray that brown baby boys become men,
Like branches on a tree that cling to the vine,
Brown babies need love now and not just sometimes.
Many are brokenhearted, broke,
Too many fallen, held back, choked,
Strangers hide from brown love, as if a disease?
Strangers threatened by brown love, spoiled?
Strangers think strange things, unknown,
Strangers fear unknown, not knowing
Strange strangers unfamiliar, black or brown man,

Alas! Light shines, through darkness,
Shines on us and within,
Our God is merciful, gives hope no matter your skin,
Our God says love each other,
Love all brothers, sisters, and all who gather.

God gives love, grace, and mercy to you and to me,
God's people are women, men, girls, boys, and babies,
All people, even strangers, are part of God's family.
All God's children, saints and sinners, Christ redeemed us all, are we.
Saved by God's Grace, one human race, twelve shades of humanity, one
God, love, people and story, one identity.

⇥ • ⇤

QUESTIONS FOR REFLECTION/ACTION

1. Take the challenge to seek out marginalized or silenced voices—their stories and their histories—with another person or group. Choose websites or media outlets that focus on a particular culture or group. Visit museums or invite presentations of silenced stories to your congregation. Pay attention to your own emotional responses to this previously unknown perspective. Are you bored or curious, uncomfortable or intrigued, ashamed or proud? Explore why you might be having these feelings.

2. We typically select our friends and associates from people of the same socioeconomic and cultural heritage. Find a small group in which you are comfortable who will intentionally reach out across these boundaries, praying and reflecting along the journey. Ask for permission to join a group of people very different from you. Check in—how do you feel, how do they feel with you present?

3. Consistently make small talk with a shopkeeper of another ethnicity, volunteer at an English as a second language class, become a big brother/sister, share fellowship with those marginally housed and fed in a free meals program (don't just cook "for" them), participate in interfaith events in your community, mentor a former inmate.

→▸ ● ◂←

Cleo D. Graham was ordained in the United Church of Christ and is author of the poetic book *From Mess to Message*. An avid writer, she has a prayer ministry and blog, Park and Pray at 1:11 PM. Pastor Cleo, an inspirational speaker, lives in Rhode Island.

M. Elizabeth Waters, known to most people as Betsy, is an ordained pastor in the United Church of Christ, having served many churches as an intentional interim or church consultant. Earlier she worked in schools as a psychologist and teacher. She prizes her three sons and six grandchildren.

3 1 ✳ RETURNING RIGHTS TO INDIGENOUS PEOPLES

An estimated five thousand Indigenous peoples are found in seventy-two countries around the world. From the Sami peoples of the Scandinavian countries and Russia to the survivors of residential schools in Canada, the United States, and Australia, cries for justice have come. From higher than average number of suicides, to land rights and appropriation of Indigenous peoples' burial lands, to confrontations in many parts of the world over habitat, resources, and ecology—a long list of challenges goes on and on.

Some Indigenous peoples have ceased to exist. No pure Ainu people of northern Japan remain—only those of mixed race. The Indigenous people of Tasmania are now extinct, their remains on display in the British Museum and other museums around the world, which resist returning them. In South America, those of western origin search out Indigenous peoples who have avoided contact, once again taking with them diseases unknown to those peoples, and depriving them of their health and way of life.

Depending on location, conditions in Indigenous communities vary from the most abominable (the town of Attawapiskat in Canada) to nearing excellent (exemplified by the Sami people, who now have their own Parliament and the right to education in their native language, although this right to self-government was only granted in 1996 after much struggle). Indigenous languages disappear as those who can speak them age and die. Canada's Indian Act remains a piece of legislation from 1876 that has been described as "entrenched paternalism," and that has changed very little over the years. Indigenous peoples are more likely to be incarcerated, and governments still practice policies of "extinguishment" of rights of Indigenous peoples.

In 2010 in the United States, President Obama signed the Tribal Law and Order Act, returning the rights of Indigenous peoples to prosecute violent crimes on their own lands. In 2016, appropriation and sale of tribal burial grounds under the law of eminent domain was overridden by President Obama. Indigenous Aboriginal peoples in Australia eventually received a formal apology from their government, and the country now celebrates "Sorry Day." Some Canadian universities now require all first-year students to take a course in Indigenous history within the country. Ashes of Australian Aboriginal individuals have at last been returned from the British Museum to the Aboriginal people of Australia.

The rights of Indigenous peoples, however, are still far from complete. Deleted from many history books, their cultures are often unknown and their struggles overridden by governing bodies with little knowledge or appreciation of these communities. While steps have been taken in some cases to give respect and autonomy to these peoples, there is still plenty of room for prayerful action, support, and education.

PERSONAL PRAYER

O Great Spirit, may the eagle carry my prayers to your listening heart. My soul is concerned for your children, my sisters and brothers. Many have lost their time-honoured ways, and turn to the ways of those who have oppressed us. Our children have lost their desire to live and do not find hope. Our traditional lands do not support us the way they did; many live in poverty and despair. Erase from our ears the sound of children crying as they were taken to residential schools, and replace it with the sound of children laughing. Remind us to be proud of our heritage and stand tall in our moccasins.

O Sacred Spirit, I ask that your joy in creation and in the interconnected web of life encourage us. May I find my delight in what you provide, the glorious colours of a hummingbird, the scent of lilacs in the spring, the cool, living waters in summer, the freshness of a fall morning, and the comfort of a crackling fire in winter. Enable us to feel connections with all indigenous people, our ancestors, and our children to come. I ask that we regain our vision and dreams. As we walk our lands with gentle feet, we greet the day with hope, and say goodnight with full hearts. Meegwetch.

COMMUNITY PRAYER

To Our Creator, a Prayer of Thankfulness

O Great Spirit, Creator of all that is full of goodness and giving,
human beings, creatures of the earth, sea, and sky,
food from fields, forest, rivers, oceans, and air,
our hearts are full of gratitude.
We have medicine plants to keep us well,
and teachings to pass onto our children.
Our Elders and Grandparents share their wisdom,
that we may be a community of people in harmony.
We celebrate your life, Spirit, in all we are and all we do.
In our time we will join in the dance of the ancestors,
lighting the sky with our brilliance and thankfulness. Amen

All My Relations

Akwe Nia'Tetewá:neren, "All my relations" in Mohawk
Mitákuye Oyás'in, "All my relations" in Lakota

The term *Mitákuye Oyás'in,* "all my relations," originated with the Lakota Nation in the United States. It is now commonly used by all Aboriginal, Inuit, and Métis people in North America. This term breathes of the sense of unity, belonging, equality, and interconnectedness of all creation. Everything that is nourished and nurtured by water, air, and soil is our relative and partner. We are all part of the interweb of life—human, creatures, and plants, We all depend on each other for our being, and all are part of the One. Nothing and no one that is alive is excluded. We are invited to see the sacred in everything. It is said with great reverence during Aboriginal ceremonies.

Mitákuye Oyás'in—all my relations. Speak these words in your community. Speak these words when you walk under the sky. Speak these words when you face those who confront you or attack you. Speak these words in your heart. Open your arms wide as you speak the words, to symbolize your embrace of all our relations in creation.

→ ▸ • ◂ ←

QUESTIONS FOR REFLECTION/ACTION

1. What do we know about Indigenous peoples? Who are they? How have they been treated by "incomers" in various places? Consider the American continents, Australia, Aotearoa, and the Pacific Islands.

2. What actions can we take in our personal lives to nurture our appreciation of Indigenous people and their culture?

3. What can we do, as a North American society, to alleviate the struggles of our First Nations/Native American youth with regards to racism, addictions, and suicide?

→ ▸ • ◂ ←

Nancy Arthur Best writes from Ontario, Canada, and has Mohawk heritage. Both Nancy and Fran are ordained clergy in the United Church of Canada, which has been deeply involved in the Truth and Reconciliation Commission, hearings around Indigenous peoples in Canada, headed by Justice Murray Sinclair, himself an Indigenous person. We use the term "Indigenous peoples" to recognize those who were present when outsiders arrived. For us, justice and restitution emerge as paramount.

Frances E. Ota is a minister in the United Church of Canada, and has an MDiv and BMusic. She is married to Professor Norio Ota, has four children and four grandchildren, and loves to garden, read, write, and pick at her Celtic harp.

32  PRAYERS FOR THE PEOPLE AND THE LAND OF ISRAEL AND PALESTINE

For generations, the people of this region have struggled to live side by side in the land many faiths call holy. This land is simultaneously a place of pilgrimage, devotion, prayer, struggle, oppression, and terror. There is much joy and celebration as people stream here to show their love for God and to await the Messiah, but year after year, as we wait, much blood is shed in the search for security, in the name of peace. We lift up these prayers, joining the cacophony of the prayers of residents, pilgrims, martyrs, and warriors. We wait for the day when kindred shall live together in unity.

Suggested Reading: Amos 9:7 and Psalms 10:17, 18

PERSONAL PRAYER

Prayer for Peace

Holy One, Avinu Shebashamayim:

Hear this prayer from the sons and daughters of Abraham, Isaac, Ishmael, Jacob, and Esau; Sarah, Hagar, Rebecca, Leah, and Rachel. Hear our prayer, O God, in our time of extremity and sorrow.

We beseech you for wisdom and clarity. We ask you to help us to find
within ourselves these truths:

That peace cannot come without justice. That you are God,
who requires justice.

That every person is your chosen, every people your chosen.

That you are God, father
and mother of all.

Tonight, we beseech our fellow men and women,
of all faiths and nationalities,
to offer up prayer—*t'fillah*—and praise—*t'hillah*.

Pray for the leaders who have forgotten their people,
who have stopped up their hearts.

Grant them the courage of Martin Luther King Jr,
of Mother Teresa, of Desmond Tutu.

Pray for the parents who protect their own but sacrifice the children
of others.

Open their hearts.

Pray for the misguided who foul water wells, poison the flocks,
and cut down olive trees.

Open their minds.

Pray for the sons and daughters, the mothers and fathers, who have
yielded to despair and lifted up the flag of hatred and annihilation.

Heal their souls and grant them peace.

Praise the steadfast and simple, the pure of spirit,
who shield the vulnerable and feed the hungry.
Praise the loyal and the liberated from greed, who love the land
and covet not the groves of their brothers and sisters.
Praise the strong and the stubborn, who defy the unjust edict
and honor the law of the Eternal.
Praise the bereaved and the brokenhearted, whose souls have reached
the very bottom of the well of loss, and from that fullness and depth
have reached up to embrace their brothers and sisters in pain and hope.
Praise the kind and the generous, the truly content in their lives of

service, who teach us devotion, who teach us love,
who light our way in the darkness.

Teach us to care, O God, teach us to care and not despair, teach us to
build your heavenly Jerusalem, and to unite our suffering divided
earthly Jerusalem.
Teach us to walk in your ways.

And in the words of your prophet Amos (5:22–24):
> Let justice well up as waters,
> and righteousness as a mighty stream.

COMMUNITY PRAYER

Creator
You knew the universe
before it was formed.
Darkness and watery chaos prevailed.
> **You spoke and**
> **separated light from darkness,**
> **water from dry land.**
Did you know how we would love the land?
> **We call it sacred, holy, promised.**
> **Mine.**
You formed the creatures of sky and earth,
birds who know no borders,
fish who know no weapons.
> **Did you know how we would separate ourselves by**
> **skin colour, ancestry, language,**
> **geography and lines on a map?**
God, you formed human beings and
gave us your breath.
> **Did you know we would**
> **sing and laugh,**
> **debate and argue,**
> **holler and cry?**

Did you know we would coo to our lover and
utter murderous threats to our neighbor?
Holy One, does your heart swell to see how hard we try to show we
love you:
We offer prayers, adoration, holy time, pilgrimage, sacrament, and service.
Does your heart break when you see how hard we strive
to demand our rights,
to protect our bodies,
to own our land,
to have dominion over one another?
Pour out your gracious mercy upon us,
forgive us, heal us.
Join us together again, as brothers and sisters,
as neighbors, as friends,
so that we may perfectly love you,
and enter into your presence with praise and thanksgiving.

Closing

Greet one another with a sign of peace saying:
"*Shalom chaverim*" or "*Al-salaamu alaykum.*"
RESPONSE: *Wa 'alykum.*

→─ • ─←

QUESTIONS FOR REFLECTION/ACTION

1. When war is ended, peace does not "break out." Peace must be
   made, deliberately and constructively with a plan of alternatives to
   the present. What are some examples of peace-making and how
   can you carry a message of peace, love, and reconciliation into situations of despair and brokenness?

2. What does the term "holy land" mean to you? Spend time
   imagining the coming together of Jews, Christians, and Muslims,
   the three peoples of the Abrahamic faiths, to work together for

justice and peace in this one land. How can you show that you strive for extravagant justice?

→➤ • ◄←

Wendy Adams is a retired minister of the Presbyterian Church in Canada. She resides in the Okanagan Valley of British Columbia on the ancestral territories and unceded lands of the Okanagan and Shushwap nations.

Mark Braverman is Jewish American with family roots in Jerusalem. He is a founder of Friends of Tent of Nations North America and serves on the advisory board of Friends of Sabeel North America and the Board of Directors of the Tree of Life Educational Foundation. He is program director for Kairos USA. Mark is the author of *Fatal Embrace: Christians, Jews, and the Search for Peace in the Holy Land* and *A Wall in Jerusalem: Hope, Healing, and the Struggle for Peace in Israel and Palestine*. Mark blogs at Patheos.org. His writings, videos, and sermons can be found at www.markbraverman.org.

33 ✳ MERCY AND TRUTH, JUSTICE AND PEACE FOR ZIMBABWE AND AFRICA

Zimbabwe, and Africa in general,
is in a phase of transition.
Years of injustice, human rights abuses,
intolerance, nepotism, internalized external oppression and corruption
are being replaced by citizen voices of democracy,
citizen activism, pro-democracy movements and demonstrations.
However, there remains a question.
Are all these movements in line with the ingredients of peace building?
Psalm 85:10 says, "Mercy and truth have met each other: justice and
    peace have kissed"
The truth is, Mother Africa has suffered for centuries.
Alas, this truth without mercy is treacherous.
International courts of justice indict African leaders and former leaders
of war crimes and gross human rights abuses.

But does this justice have mercy?
Does it have truth?
If so, which truth?
We all need peace!
Some believe peace through armed struggle and terrorism,
some through nonviolent struggle.
Does this take acquaintance of the ingredients of peace building?
Africa needs peace building ingredients today more than ever before.
These are the ingredients from David, the great psalmist:
Mercy
Truth
Justice
Peace!

PERSONAL PRAYER

FROM PSALM 85 *by Maren Tirabassi*

God, I run away from Truth
and from people I know
who have not told it in the past.
I handle Mercy with a credit card
and not with my hands.
I become cynical, believing Justice
is always trumped by self-interest.
I despair when Peace is trampled
by people of faith—traditional,
Muslim and Christian.
Up from the ground of Africa,
down from the bright sky,
come, O God, now,
and help me to believe
in your Kiss—the Kiss of God
that will restore and revive
all of your people. Amen

COMMUNITY PRAYER

A Prayer for the Countries of Africa

[Check the current status before engaging this prayer]

Many people who do not live in Africa do not know the names of the countries there, or they know names but do not know the countries' history, landscape, language, concerns, even location.

Simplest Prayer

The leader reads each name and, after the country name (knowing it stands for the land, history, all of God's children and God's creatures who live there), the group responds: "Mercy and Truth, Justice and Peace."

We begin to pray by saying the names:

Algeria, Angola, Benin, Botswana, Burkina Faso, Burundi, Cabo Verde, Cameroon, Central African Republic, Chad, Comoros, Cote d'Ivoire, Democratic Republic of the Congo (Kinshasa, formerly Zaire), Djibouti, Egypt, Equatorial Guinea, Eritrea, Ethiopia, Gabon, Gambia, Ghana, Guinea Bissau, Guinea, Kenya, Lesotho, Liberia, Libya, Madagascar, Malawi, Mali, Mauritania, Mauritius, Morocco, Mozambique, Namibia, Niger, Nigeria, Republic of the Congo (Brazzaville), Réunion, Rwanda, Sénégal, Seychelles, Sierra Leone, Sao Tome & Principe, Somalia, South Africa, Sudan, Swaziland, Tanzania, Togo, Tunisia, Uganda, Western Sahara, Zambia, Zanzibar, Zimbabwe.

A Prayer of Intercession

Identify five countries in Africa highlighted in an African news site (perhaps sharing that there is such a thing). A country could be recovering from a natural disaster, waiting for an impending election, suffering a major conflict or an epidemic, or celebrating a world honor. Ask five people to learn and share why these countries need prayer. After the descriptions, the leader names each country in turn and people speak aloud prayers for that country—from their new knowledge or in general, such as "I pray for the children of _____ , I thank God for the beauty of

_____ , May there be peace between different peoples, traditionally enemies, who must live together in _____ . Amen."

→⊳ • ⊲←

QUESTIONS FOR REFLECTION/ACTION

These questions are often a part of the exercises that Lance leads throughout Africa, training people to be reconcilers and peacemakers in their communities.

1. If you were given the choice between truth, mercy, justice, or peace, what would you pick?

2. What would your chosen quality be like if it took shape in a person today?

3. What would be the message that quality/person would give?

4. What would happen if that message were ignored?

5. Which of the other three is your best ally? Why?

6. Which of the other three gives you the most trouble? Why?

→⊳ • ⊲←

Lance Muteyo is a Zimbabwean-born Christian peacemaker, environmentalist, writer, and performing poet. He is married to Christina. Lance has travelled to many African and European countries facilitating workshops in conflict transformation and environmental activism. He mainly works with children and young people.

34 CHILDREN AND MIGRATION

Between 2013 and 2014, the number of children crossing the U.S.-Mexico border increased dramatically. Child migrants do not get as much attention as adults in the media but, according to UNICEF, there at least sixty-five million children around the world who are on the move. They are fleeing from violence and conflict in their home countries. Sometimes they are running to escape poverty or extreme climate change. Everywhere they are looking for a home and a better life from the ones they are enduring every day. Every year, every month, situations change, but children are always on the move and they are vulnerable.

Migrants in Britain in 2016 are worried about the future of their children after Britain's decision to break away from the European Union. Immigrants without documentation with children born in the United States are filled with fear as new legislation looms on the horizon. There are many people on the ground working to make things better for child migrants. They are aware that children on the move are constantly in danger of exploitation and abuse. Go to UNICEF.org or find an organization near you and volunteer to do something for children on the move in places like Central America, Europe, Nigeria, Tanzania, Yemen, Burundi, and the Syrian Arab Republic.

PERSONAL PRAYER

Holy One, Father and Mother of us all, listen to the voices of the children, those who are sometimes too young to understand what is going on in the world around them, those who are too young to comprehend why the world has been so cruel to those most vulnerable. Amen

PRAYER *by Todd Jenkins*

Hear my prayer, O holy one,
as I stare children in the face,
yearning to find a sacred space
where your will for them may be done.
Since angst was wed to nation-state,
Love has taken second chair.
Violence is always there,
at the corner of Fear and Hate.
When children hail from different places
we erase their gift of humanity,
and take away their dignity,
seeing no resemblance in their faces.
"Send them back!" we hear the scream.
"Protect our sacred real estate
by any means, including hate;
give them a nightmare for their dream."
"How dare their parents let them go!"
Unable to fathom, with feigned confusion
pogo-sticking to conclusion
as if we somehow really know.
When we haven't faced circumstances
of utterly hopeless brutality,
with no real hope or hospitality,
we can't imagine taking those chances.
Truth these children are bearing
can only help our hearts transform
if, steeped as tea, from hot to warm,
we hear the stories they are sharing.

COMMUNITY PRAYER

Forgive us, O God, when we refuse to offer welcome to the alien and the stranger, the asylum seeker and the stateless refugee, and those who are displaced by war or famine. We call on you, as one who sets captives free, that you would gently open the doors of our homes and our hearts to all people in need,

Bless your children, O God, and bring laughter and hope into their lives. May we wake up to a new world where justice and peace will reign in our land. May it be so. Amen

LITANY FOR TRAVELING CHILDREN (PSALM 85:10) *by Maren Tirabassi*

For children who flee bombs falling across waters where others have drowned, past boundaries of razor wire.

RESPONSE: **May an open heart and an open home meet; may hope and happiness hold hands.**

For children who journey alone, seeking family who have gone ahead, fearing being caught and sent back to death or poverty.

(RESPONSE)

For children who travel with the seasons of fruit and vegetables, visiting school after school, clinic after clinic, local library, ball field, playground—longing for welcome.

(RESPONSE)

For children who are left with many siblings and one stressed parent when the other is deported, who may be filled with grief or anger, fear or confusion.

(RESPONSE)

For minors whose childhood has been stolen, who run from gang recruitment, forced child soldiering, child marriage, abusive labor practices.

(RESPONSE)

For citizen teens trying to fulfill their parents' dream of being U.S. educated and to make the rent when both parents are stuck in immigrant detention fighting their cases for months.

(RESPONSE)

For children who know they are athletes, artists, poets, mathematicians, musicians, and who need nurture to share their gifts.

(RESPONSE)

For children who love their heritage, wish their parents would lighten up about it a little, and just want to fit in with new friends.

(RESPONSE)

⤙ • ⤚

QUESTIONS FOR REFLECTION/ACTION

1. Why do people migrate? Why do children migrate? What might they be running away from? What are they hoping will happen in the new land?

2. How are their hopes also our hopes? How is their suffering also ours?

3. What are the many ways we exclude children, in our homes, our schools, our churches? Which of these ways are intentional and which are unintentional?

⤙ • ⤚

Rafael Vallejo started his theological education at the Graduate Theological Union in Berkeley and San Francisco Theological Seminary in San Anselmo, California, and completed his MDiv in Canada at the Toronto School of Theology. He was a chef by trade before he answered the call to ministry.

35 ✳ THE INVISIBLE WORLD OF MIGRANT AGRICULTURAL WORKERS

In the United States, most of the fresh produce available in grocery stores is planted, cultivated, and harvested by migrants. Many of these agricultural workers come from Central American nations, crossing the southern U.S. border, often without documentation. Their lives swing in the precarious balance between corporations and farm owners focused on profits, and governments acknowledging neither the policies forcing their migration nor the systemic invisibility and exploitation of both workers and their families. As international governments enact more "free trade" agreements, the means and opportunities for laborers to provide basic necessities for themselves and their families shrink, ramping up pressure for economic-driven migration and family separation.

PERSONAL PRAYER

LIBERTY

Migrant workers give the privileged
tomatoes, peppers, hybrid melons,
yearning to be consumed,

at the expense of tired, poor,
coyote-herded masses
dying to breathe free.

The wretched refuse of bowing
to chemicals and corporations
has USA's shores teeming with toxicity,
and hearts quivering with xenophobia.

The tempest-tossed and border-crossed,
who dream of hope
have not so much been met
with lamp at shining door,
as laser sight and incarceration.

Is it consumptive greed,
blind eye turned to the duplicity
of deportation and the rending
of family's fabric, to which
undying allegiance is claimed?

Liberty, though, has long-slipped by
the now-empty tomb's ill-fitting millstone.
She dances in the hearts
of children and grandchildren
as they, tender-hearted and innocent,
sit next to one another in school,
sing beside each other in worship,
grow up and vote with their faith
and not their fears.

With eyes and hearts wide open,
filled by the hope of our eternal oneness,
anxiety cannot and will not
stand in the light of grace.

COMMUNITY PRAYER

Litany for Sacred Labor (Leviticus 19:33–34)

ONE: Hear Moses' words to a wilderness nation: "When an alien resides with you in your land, you shall not oppress the alien."

MANY: The alien who resides with you shall be to you as the citizen among you; you shall love the alien as yourself, for you were aliens in the land of Egypt.

ONE: In the call of its priestly leaders, the newly forming nation of Israel receives a divine reminder of its wandering roots.

MANY: Let us also remember the many ways our own ancestors traveled across continents, oceans, or generations in search of resources to provide for families.

ONE: From the beginning, creation's gifts have sustained us all.

MANY: Our journeys and arrivals have been grounded in the strong and tender hand of God's grace.

ONE: Let us not allow fear to grow from the branch of difference.

MANY: May we, instead, claim the common roots of our humanity, recognizing diversity as an essential part of creation's blueprint.

ONE: The universe is a neighborhood into which we've been poured.

MANY: Fear convinces us to shrink, control, protect, and gate our lives.

ONE: Grace welcomes us to expand, release, free, and open ourselves to love.

MANY: The former choice leads to the creation of enemies and despair; the latter, to the creation of neighbors and hope.

ONE: When people are used and things are loved, we become tight-fisted possessives of our possessions, and our fearful exclamation is, "There goes the neighborhood!"

MANY: When people are loved and things are used, we are able to become gently holding stewards of possessions, and our joyful exclamation is, "Here comes our neighbor!"

ONE: We pray this day for all who labor and are heavily burdened; for heads of household who must travel great distances and struggle to feed their families on insufficient wages earned far from home.

MANY: **We pray for migrant workers whose lives are shortened by the market's brutal disregard for their health, and for the fabric of family torn asunder by profit-driven forces.**

ONE: Make us instruments of specific and hopeful change in individual and corporate circumstances, O God.

MANY: **Give us the courage and tenacity to create a world where worth, compensation, and dignity are determined not by birth certificate, nationality, or language, but by labor, our common bond of humanity, and God's unmerited grace.**

ALL: **May we find ways to keep our palms upturned and opened, O God, so we can freely receive and give your gifts with joy and generosity, as you guide us through the nudging of your Holy Spirit. Amen**

⟶ • ⟵

QUESTIONS FOR REFLECTION/ACTION

1. Where can you find out more about people in your community whose struggles are intrinsically tied to immigration and labor policies?

2. What can you and your faith community do to help individuals who are struggling because of low wages and families who are separated by work's limited availability?

3. How can you, at a systemic level, advocate for immigration policies and labor laws that give workers a fair wage and an opportunity to remain connected to their families?

4. What gifts do immigrants bring to your community—music, art, wisdom from their heritage, food—and how might you encourage the sharing of these gifts with appreciation and respect?

⟶ • ⟵

J. Todd Jenkins is a Presbyterian Church USA pastor in Tennessee who enjoys hiking with his wife, running, cooking, and combining prayer and poetry into prayetry.

36 ✳ SNAPPY MEALS FROM A CROCK POT SYSTEM
ISSUES OF LABOR JUSTICE

How long is a drive-through order guaranteed at McDonalds? Sixty seconds. How long did it take for fast-food workers to receive a living wage? We're still waiting. This is why some time ago, before there was a "Fight-for-$15" movement, I found myself in a room with other seminarians, activists, and clergy. "The Black Institute," "United NY," "NY Communities for Change," fast-food workers, the 1199 SEIU Labor Union, my colleagues at the Judson Memorial Church, and a small number of faith leaders who were sick and tired of workers working and still not being able to thrive got together. Some of us woke up as early as 3:30 A.M. to engage in a coordinated citywide day-of-action in New York City. The synergy of fear and courage sparked something within me that day to making this work a priority.

Some years later, we live in a time where we've seen the first "Fight-For-$15" National Convention in Richmond, Virginia. We live in an age where social media, fast food, and food technology continue to boom. One might think, as this kind of progress has taken place, that treatment of workers would advance. However, fast-food workers are still receiving "Crock Pot Justice."

Food prepared in a crock-pot takes a long time to be ready for consumption. It takes hours to see that the meal is actually being cooked. The average adult fast-food worker with a child needs to work full-time at an hourly rate of $20.86 (an unheard of wage) just to afford the basics of survival (food, clothing, and shelter). There are many times when workers report to work sick, putting customers at risk, because they are not given paid sick days. In order for workers to earn as much as a CEO they would need to work a total of one-million hours a year. Last, but not least, when workers try to organize or engage in active, courageous, nonviolent dialogue with their employers to demand a living wage, they often face fear of termination from their employer or they outright lose their jobs.

Meals are guaranteed in less than three minutes and yet justice seems to barely have begun cooking. God's table is one where all are treated with love and compassion. Faith communities organize and speak out for the rights of workers. Change is on the horizon. My prophetic cry is for workers to have the courage to resist unjust wages, claiming their place at the table for all. We still have work to do and a long way to go.

PERSONAL PRAYER

Serving God,
May the hands and feet of workers discover the courage to move from the assembly line to the protest line. May spatulas be exchanged for pickets, doubts exchanged for assurances in the struggle for justice through the power of collective action. Amen

COMMUNITY PRAYER

LITURGICAL RESOURCES FOR WORKER JUSTICE SUNDAY

Call to Worship (Matthew 11:28)

ONE: Jesus says, "Come to me"

MANY: **All who labor.**

ONE: Jesus says, "Come to me"

MANY: **All who are weary.**

ONE: Jesus says "Come to me"

MANY: All who fiercely resist evil and oppression.

ONE: Jesus says "Come to me"

ALL: I will give you rest, I will give you justice, and I will give you freedom.

Opening Prayer

May our courage to fight for a living wage
Shine bright as the moon in the midnight sky
May the sound of our voices
Reach the peak of the highest skyscraper
And the depths of the lowest valley
May the movement of our hands and feet
Be felt in the boardroom
And celebrated in the throne room
Moving from the assembly line to the picket line
Enveloped in God's care.
Secured by God's call
Making a place at the table for all. Amen

Call to Confession

We confess there have been times where we have been filled with fear, an unholy fear that consumes us. Fear has invited us to place self-interest before the common good. Fear of opposition has caused us to be silent. Fear of criticism has paralyzed us from moving our feet for justice. Fear of failure has kept us from being our best self, reflected in the perfect example of nonviolent resistance—Jesus Christ. Transform our fear into courage like the barren field whose soil has been nurtured and embodies the beauty of the earth.

Assurance of Grace

As we resist fear, God offers us courage.
When we risk something big for something good, God offers us hope.
As we exchange comfort for agitation, God offers us celebration.
Giving up our guilt, we can embrace God's amazing grace.

Suggested Gospel Lesson for Worker Justice Sunday: Matthew 20:1–16

Commentary

It is just one of those days. The day begins really early and finishes really late. Returning home to the parsonage, I park my car in the garage and grudgingly walk up the stairs. I turn the corner in the kitchen and walk up the next flight of stairs. Everything I would need from the car is in hand to prevent having to make an extra trip back down and up those stairs. I lie in bed only to be startled by a sudden piercing ring in my ears. It is the smoke alarm.

I am filled with a wave of fear that either fire is coming or carbon monoxide will silently enter my system as I sleep. The procession down the first flight of stairs is tolerable. No sign of smoke anywhere. I grab the smoke detector from the wall since it will not stop beeping. Nothing seems to stop the sound. The next day I speak with a trustee, who tells me, "It's not what you think—it just needs new batteries!" Fear filled me over nothing.

Such a text is quite fitting when we think about labor and the economy. We hear the noise—the annals of modern capitalism teaches profit as more valuable than people. Those who have the means to gain more capital are entitled to it because they earned it. We hear the noise—the assumption that the "first," the individual who built the corporation, who has labored in the proverbial vineyard, is entitled to more. We hear the noise—the "last," those who labor with less-than-acceptable means, deserve their plight of having less. We hear the noise—and it should fill us with that bolt of fear.

This parable radically transforms how we are invited to think about the economy. What we've heard might not be what we first imagine. The owner of the estate puts the needs of the workers first. A typical day's wage during that time was worth about twenty cents in silver (Tob. 5:14). If it was agreed upon verbally, it was binding by law. Although some of these workers didn't spend the whole day in the vineyard, the estate owner sees their need and pays all of them for an entire day's work.

The economy of the Spirit is quite contrary to our own. God's economy invites us to think about the common good, about those who are seen as the least, and about making the human condition a paramount concern over profit.

Benediction

May justice rise to meet you
May the urgency of now always be on your back
May the hope for an economy that cares for all people warm upon your
　　face
and rains of a transformed world fall soft upon your fields
And until we meet again, May God hold you in the palm of God's just
　　hand.

→→ • ←←

QUESTIONS FOR REFLECTION/ACTION

1. Has there ever been a time when you witnessed work-related injustice? How have you responded? What do you believe Jesus would do?

2. What other parts of your faith tradition inspire you to believe that justice for all workers is not optional, but necessary?

3. How do you feel when you think about engaging in the struggle for worker justice? What does that look like for you?

→→ • ←←

Eric C. Jackson is pastor of Brookside Congregational Church, UCC, in Manchester, New Hampshire, and is currently pursuing a Doctor of Ministry at Hartford Seminary. Eric is passionate about the future of the mainline church, acquiring new fountain pens, and enjoying spirited conversations about the world to come over delicious coffee at postmodern cafes.

37 ✳ SANCTUARY
ADEQUATE FOOD, SHELTER, AND SAFETY

Jesus was homeless. Jesus tells the scribe this—that he is without a place to lay his head—after the scribe tells him, "I will follow you wherever you go."

Following Jesus means going to places where people live in cars, under bridges, in tents next to busy freeways.

Following Jesus means being present to those who have nowhere to lay their head . . . because the family fled barrel bombs on a night with no visible stars . . . because she left through a window at midnight after her partner broke her ribs . . . because he is working two jobs and still cannot afford rent for his family . . .

Jesus tells us too that whatever we do for the least of these, we have done for him (Matt. 25:40). The Son of Man had nowhere to lay his head, but we can make a place for the people who stand in front of us today to claim as home. The Son of Man knew long days of hunger, but we can feed those who are present to us today in their hunger and thirst. The Son of Man knew what it was to stand alone on edges, but we can go to the edges of today and pull people in to a new community where all are welcome, all are fed, all are invited to feast on God's abundance.

PERSONAL PRAYER

God-among-us,

You came into a fragile time, and lived without enough.
You intimately knew the way that hunger can impale a person,
That brown dust can mark skin for days without being washed off.
You knew what it was to live under hot Judean sun
With no cover,
And what it was to feel lashes on your back.
And you testified,
Over and over,
That there could be a different way.
You taught us to take the loaves and fishes of each day,
And to stand on hillsides and break them open
To feed others.
You taught us to get close enough to each other
To be healed by one another.
You taught us that we can
Be the builders of sanctuaries,
And that we can be your
Sacred shelter,
Your succor,
Your enough,
For one another.
Amen

Suggested Reading—2 Corinthians 9:12

God of plenty, your storehouses are overflowing, but there are so many hungry here. Young and old seek nourishment. Young and old have cupboards full. Teach us to fill the gap and fill everyone's cup with your overflowing mercy.
Amen

Sanctuary —Suggested Reading Psalm 91:1

There is nothing insane about wanting sanctuary. But in this crazy world, many lack the sanity of shelter.

Some people relate shelter to a physical object—tent, tarp, house, vehicle, coat, or box. Others think of shelter from criticism, hatred, hunger, prejudice, nature, holidays, depression, anxiety, addiction, and expectations.

We often forget those few blessed souls who have learned to live in the ideal sanctuary of mental, physical, and spiritual shelter in the Trinity.

For those blessed with holy refuge, the challenge and responsibility is teaching others the path—educating so others may also live in compassion.

A safe shelter is offered to all by Jesus. And if we truly live for Jesus, we will seek to make sanctuary available to all.

COMMUNITY PRAYER

A CYCLE

A habit that continues
And thrives through war and peace
Infecting our universe
A cycle of poverty
Poverty of living in the absence of mercy
Of living in the want of acceptance
Of living in the void of laughter
Poverty that closes our hearts
To the need of others
To the battle for mere existence
Where Souls struggle
Poverty that blinds our senses
Our view of right and
Takes us to a self-righteous place
A cycle of poverty
That survives
And spreads like fungus
In the dark, stinking corners of our minds
Until an exchange makes a crack
Light creeps in the fissure
And change begins

A cycle that is centuries old
Finds a new path
A path of planting support,
Nourishment, safety, and God
A new cycle

Prayer of Confession

God of the Loaves and the Fish, God of Abundance,
    you give us enough.
You created the earth with enough for all, if we use it as you intend.
We confess that we have chosen not to fully commit with our lives.
We confess that we have chosen the ease of charity over the
    steep climb of justice, giving a little bit over changing all.
We know that Jesus said, "Foxes have dens and birds have nests,
but I have no place to lay my head."
May we hear an invitation to turn our lives.
May we hear a call to go out,
to be the makers of sanctuaries,
to be the prophets of God's Enough,
to be the ones who pray more than words, pray with our lives.

Assurance of Grace

The God of Loaves and Fish teaches us how to share slices of hope, how
to stand on the shore with those who have little and cast a line together.

→- • -←

QUESTIONS FOR REFLECTION/ACTION

1. Jesus did not heal and impact people only at a distance. He got
close to people and was changed by them. Have you heard the story
of someone without sanctuary? If so, how did hearing the story
impact you? How would that be different if you encountered
personally someone without a home, without safety?

2. How do you feel God calling you to work for justice, beyond financial charity?

3. What are some specific steps you can take in your life to bring about the world God intends? Can you invite others in your faith community to take those steps with you?

→→ • ←←

Arlene L. Drennan is a native Iowan, raised in the rich heartland of farming. Her church life has its core in a small rural church. She is a commissioned minister for the Church of Christ—Disciples of Christ in the Upper Midwest. She's never known hunger or abuse.

Laura Martin is an authorized minister in the United Church of Christ. She worked in homeless services for thirteen years and met many women, men, and children who had experienced insecurity, abuse, war, and lack of sanctuary. She's been deeply impacted by their testimonies in words and in their lives.

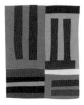

38 ✳ STREET MINISTRY
OUTSIDE OUR PEWS

We participate in a local street ministry on Sunday afternoons. We see many people who love Jesus but would not cross the thresholds of most churches because the gap, usually beginning with economics, is too vast between the people on the street and the people in the church, in spite of the latter's expressed welcome.

The people on the street have experienced and continue to experience trauma. Their trauma can be attributed to any number of factors—addiction, mental illness, loss of a loved one, PTSD, domestic abuse, loss of employment, underemployment, a lack of affordable housing—the list goes on. They have often been rejected by their families and other church communities. They struggle to see God's love reflected in those they meet for any number of legitimate reasons.

PERSONAL PRAYER

OUTRAGEOUS (OR WHY I CAN'T WALK THROUGH THE DOORS OF THE CHURCH)

You think I'm outrageous
Because my rage is visible
It is coming out of my pores
You don't want to see me

Because I make you uncomfortable
"There but for the grace of God go I"
I am you in different circumstances
You are afraid and I am outraged

Please see me
Hear my story
Help me voice my rage and my sorrow
And I will do the same for you

SURRENDER

hey God—

people are always
telling me I should
make different choices

so patronizing

or at least I should
consider making
different choices

blah, blah, blah

see, there are
so many things
I need to think about
when I make a decision
that I can't say out loud

when I forget
things don't go well

let me count the times

so I am holding
on for dear life

white-knuckling it

but I am so tired

maybe I can relax
my hands just enough
to let the color return

unclench my jaw

take a breath

can you meet me there?

COMMUNITY PRAYER

Responsive Call to Worship

ONE: As we gather here today, our hearts are aflame with our yearning to belong.

MANY: **Come, Holy Spirit, come.**

ONE: Our tongues are aflame with thoughts and stories to be shared.

MANY: **Come, Holy Spirit, come.**

ONE: Yet we hesitate to welcome. Our ears are blocked by our own experiences.

ALL: **Come, Holy Spirit, come. Like those gathered for Pentecost long ago, allow us to hear and understand each other. Gather us into beloved community. Amen**

Litany

Loving and merciful God, your compassion knows no bounds. You are a source of hope for people whose lives are a constant struggle. You love us, even when we don't feel we are loved. You know our names. We pray for those in our community who need your love and compassion. We pray that you give them strength for their days. We pray that you shine a light to dispel their darkness and give them hope to end their anxiety.

We pray for Ken, who struggles with his addictions. He lost his home and his family. Help him in his recovery, which is day by day. We need to know Ken,

Because Ken is our neighbor.

We pray for Julie, a single mom who lost her job and without work couldn't support her children. They went into foster care. She cries every day and wants to work so she can get them back. We need to know Julie,

Because Julie is our neighbor.

We pray for Barney, a veteran with PTSD. He drinks a lot. He can't go to the shelter. People shun him because of his rage. We need to know Barney,

Because Barney is our neighbor.

We pray for Beth. She fights the voices in her head every day. They make her ill. She says they drive her crazy. We need to know Beth,

Because Beth is our neighbor.

We pray for Steve. He just got out of a house of correction for the fifth time. He says he was wrongfully accused. His wife won't take him back. He is angry and no one will hire him. We need to know Steve,

Because Steve is our neighbor.

We pray for Annie. Every day she walks her baby in a stroller. She loves her baby, talks to her, shows her off. Her baby is a doll. We need to know Annie.

Because Annie is our neighbor,

We pray for Susan. She was raped as a teenager. Her husband physically abused her. She ran away. She shoots heroin. We need to know Susan,

Because Susan is our neighbor.

We pray for Carl. He had a business in town. He lost it in the recession. His husband kicked him out because he drank too much. No one wants to hire him. We need to know Carl,

Because Carl is our neighbor.

Though our neighbors won't sit next to us in our pew, help us, O God, to sit next to them. Prod us to leave our building to sit with our neighbor. Open our ears to hear their stories. Give us strength to help bear their stories. Open our hearts that we might love them as Jesus would. Amen

Confession Activity (John 21:15–19)

[Can be used as a children's story or activity at outdoor worship]

Reflect on how Jesus' invitation to Peter to declare his love for him allowed them to repair their relationship. Acknowledge that you are kept awake at night remembering times you have hurt others. Using a white board and dry erase markers, invite all present to make a squiggle on the board if they have ever broken a promise, hurt someone they love or looked past someone in need. Then, pass the board around again and invite all to erase their own or another's squiggle to represent God's forgiveness and always having the chance to try again.

Prayer

O Loving God, help me remember that you have already forgiven me. Knowing that, help me to do the hard work of forgiving myself. Then, enable and empower me to share your love and forgiveness with everyone I meet. Amen

→► • ◄←

QUESTIONS FOR REFLECTION/ACTION

1. How often do you consider others' stories when you are confused or upset by their behavior?

2. The situations described above are not only found among people who live in poverty. These individuals may live on your block or be in your workplace. Will these stories change the way you understand people's struggles?

3. How does poverty's presence shift the way you relate to people? What is your understanding of some of the systemic issues that contribute to persistent poverty?

4. How effectively does your church work to help any of these people? How will these stories change your church's ministry or simply your personal behavior?

➤ • ◄

Quentin Chin cooks, sings, and plays violin (functionally), which helps him serve as a chaplain at a shelter for homeless veterans.

When **Becky Crane** is not busy as a clinical social worker or engaged in street ministry, she can be found in the woods looking for poems.

39  COMMODIFICATION OR COMMUNION
LAND, ANIMALS, AND ECOSYSTEMS IN OUR FOOD CHAIN

When what God gives as a gift becomes valued only for profit and production, our communion with God's good earth is less than holy. The children of Israel walk out of Egypt into the wilderness—a food desert. The wilderness does not readily reveal its gifts. Intentional time and mindfulness must be spent immersed in the wilderness to know its gifts. Dwelling in the wilderness, a food desert, we learn that insect larvae are revealed as "manna," we learn the migration patterns of quail and the particular place where rock might be struck to find water. We learn the abundance of locusts and wild honey.

Always threatened by imperial practices of domination and subjugation, the Jewish experience of wilderness became part of their spiritual fabric. Intentional food practice, then, begins as one of the fundamental forms of identity for Jewish, Muslim, and Christian people. When food practice becomes "mindless," the land, animals, and all of creation become objects whose exploitation we justify by profit margin.

"Food desert" has quite a different meaning now. While there are many ways to define a food desert, the Healthy Food Financing Initiative

Working Group considers a food desert as a low-income census tract where a substantial number or share of residents has low access to a supermarket or large grocery store. There is food available, but it is not healthy. Or residents have not received the education to know where healthy food might be found. Many people are conditioned by advertising or group behavior patterns to eat that which is barely food and to be distanced from issues of land animals and ecosystems in the food chain.

PERSONAL PRAYER

My heart beats faster when I realize that, by solving the problems of our earth and my neighbor, I may very well be solving the problems that are before me. As our planet, our earth, is healthy, so I am healthy. As I am healthy, so our planet, our earth, is healthy. Forgive me for believing that I could exploit one at the health of the other. Help me to find the harmony you intend, so that like a beautiful melody I might sing one of so many different notes in a way that gives glory and honor to the splendor and abundance you intend. Amen

COMMUNITY PRAYERS

Prayers of People Who Seek Food Justice

Good and gracious God, you are asking us to see the earth as you do—as so very, very good: trees with fruit, bursting with seed; green plants for food, for humans and for every living creature; as a holy place for everything that breathes and to whom you have given life. We live now in a time of barrenness and winter. But we know, even though our supermarkets are full, others struggle with drought, famine, and hunger. Make us mindful of how we might live faithfully in the wilderness so that we are not dependent on unjust systems and structures that widen pain and deepen hunger. May our fasting help us to experience true feasting. Amen

We seek to be faithful, God, not only as individuals, but as a community and as your church. How do we begin this journey when we feel so fragmented, when all of our efforts seem so scattered? Gather us up, Good and Gracious God, and hold us together. Do not let us be cut off from you or from one another. Make our efforts, which often feel so small, something with meaning and difference not only for ourselves but for this good earth you have given us. Amen

A Dialogue for a Communion Morning

ONE: We bring before God the needs of the world.
Food is a primary need, a way of providing sacrament,
a way to connect us to one another.

ALL: And yet, those Twinkies look really good!
Coke is the taste that refreshes. It's the real thing!

ONE: We give thanks for the good food that comes from the earth!
How the different colors entice toward health and well-being.

ALL: I'm stuffed! Do you have any more of that peanut butter pie?
Or maybe we could heat up some of those chicken nuggets?

ONE: God has given us this food as if our lives depended on it.
How do we honor these gifts in a way that brings life and wholeness?
How do we begin to eat with intention and conscience?

ALL: Super-size me! And make sure the fries are fresh.
I love McDonald's fries.
My favorite is Arby's because they have the meats!

ONE: So let us gather with a sense of the measure and value of food.
May we eat it slowly and joyfully.
May we become a sacrament as we share the good gifts of God,
the labor of workers, the time and hands that prepare our daily bread.

Responsive Reading

ONE: There is an old monastic saying that goes: you can tell the way a person prays by the way they sweep the cloister.

ALL: Small, simple acts—repeated and repeated—done faithfully over a long period of time—eating, shopping, speaking out— reveal our character.

ONE: So as people of faith, we recognize the need for spiritual practice: small acts done regularly, consistently, persistently.

ALL: As people of faith, we seek not only our own health, but the health of our families, communities, ecosystems, and earth.

ONE: We solve for pattern.
We seek solutions that are healthy and whole for larger patterns.

ALL: A good solution is in harmony with larger patterns.
It is reciprocal, mutual, and responds to patterns of organ, organism, and ecosystem.

ONE: We are children of God. We are the body of Christ.
Our lives are lived out of a community of hope.

ALL: Small, simple acts lived out in the context of community
Bring about unexpected courage.

An Affirmation of Taste

ONE: We believe in the abundance that God provides.

ALL: An overflowing God provides for the regeneration
of the earth in all of its beautiful diversity.

ONE: And God provides real food for the nurturing of our bodies.

ALL: Even in the wilderness of life, it is God's will
that we be sustained.
We need only eyes to see the goodness intended.
We need only hearts to share and distribute.

ONE: So that the whole earth might break forth in abundance
and reveal God's kindness, we live out the questions of our faith:

ALL: What does it mean to be faithful?
What is beneficial for the whole of the earth,
the whole of our community?
What builds up the soil, the ecosystem, our bodies,
our community, our planet?

ONE: In living out the questions, God's shalom sustains
and nurtures all of us.

ALL: And we become God's joy.

⇥ • ⇤

QUESTIONS FOR REFLECTION/ACTION

1. How do our individual food choices reflect our values?

2. With rampant obesity and the advent of type 2 diabetes among children in some of the wealthiest countries of the world, what local or community initiatives would create better practices around intention and mindfulness in our food practices? Are there any foods from which our communities should fast?

3. What international action in food policy would lead to the joy and laughter of our children? How will you act to bring about this food policy?

4. How do we begin to eat with intention and conscience?

⇥ • ⇤

Michael S. Mulberry is the father of three bright and well-adjusted children: Jacob, Abraham, and Sophia. He is married to the wonderful, strong, and vivacious Rev. Tracy Heilman. He, himself, is friendly.

40 ✳ "JUST" WATER

Water is among the world's most basic needs. Every day, every creature needs water. And yet, we must ask what kinds of communities have access to clean water and which ones do not. How much does it cost? Is it safe and clean, or might it poison our crops and our bodies? Water is a matter of justice—"just" water.

North Americans were scandalized and shocked when it was revealed that the water in the pipes in the city of Flint, Michigan, was heavily polluted with lead and other damaging components. We learned that this happened when the city, trying to save money, began to pipe water from the Flint River instead of its usual supply. The Flint River water contained untreated corrosive elements and was leaching lead from the old pipes through which it went to every home. It was scandalous because people who had raised the alarm about this for months had been ignored and silenced.

Similarly, First Nations lands in Canada have been found to have had their water supplies tainted by nearby mining. Any town near strip mining, mountaintop removal, "fracking," or uranium and other heavy metal mining experiences the same concerns. Water supplies are threatened, and those who bring up the issue are silenced.

Meanwhile, in the warmer half of the earth, daily water has always been an issue in a way temperate zone dwellers can hardly understand. Children walk miles every day to bring home a gallon or two, which will be the whole family's daily supply. Crops that depend on rainfall are at increasing risk, given the complexity of climate change. And, in but one example of human injustice rather than natural factors, Palestinians in the West Bank have long lifted up the issue of their water supplies being diverted for use in unauthorized Jewish settlements.

We are people who have claimed by baptism our faith in Jesus, the one who told the Samaritan woman, "I would give you living water" (John 4:14). We are moved to pray about water and rejoice when our prayers combine with our actions to fulfill Isaiah's image.

Suggested Reading: Isaiah 44:3–4

PERSONAL PRAYER

Gracious God,

we are so thankful for the gift of water that refreshes us every new day. Fresh and clean water is like your love and presence: we need it every day of life.

God, we pray for those who don't have regular access to clean water and for those who have to walk miles to get it;

we pray for those fleeing areas where there is only dryness or drought, areas where nothing can grow and nothing can be harvested;

we pray for those living in areas where there are heavy rains and floods, areas where people lose their homes and the fields are destroyed by the floods;

we pray for those who have to walk far distances every day to get clean water;

and we pray for those who can't afford to buy clean water and are suffering under diseases because of drinking unsafe and polluted water.

Gracious God, we are thankful when we can satisfy our thirst every day with clean water;

we are thankful for every initiative that gives respect to clean water as a main resource of our life;

we are thankful for every project bringing clean, safe, and affordable water to the poor;

we are thankful for the power of the women who every day carry water long distances for the survival of their families;

we are thankful for all initiatives worldwide struggling for the access to clean water as a human right;

Gracious God, we pray for us to use our resources of clean and safe water in a conserving and saving way day by day.

Amen

COMMUNITY PRAYER

(based on John 4:1–42)

When a woman goes to the well at noon, we know she has been pushed to the margins by her neighbors' disapproval. We pray, dear God, for all those whom we have sent away by our disapproving looks, our shaking heads. Push us by your Holy Spirit to stretch our hands out in welcome, extravagant welcome, even to those who make us squirm.

When Jesus asks for a cup of water, we know he is breaking the rules, talking to a woman of Samaria. We pray, dear God, for such courage to break unjust rules. Make us not afraid to ask for a cup of water from those the world does not expect will give it.

We, too, long for your living water, O Christ. With the insistent woman we ask, "Give us this water, so we may never be thirsty." Give us the water that will become in us a spring of water gushing up to eternal life.

Splash us with wake-up juice. Shower us with reassurance. Lead us into the waves unafraid. Show us how, in our time, you are calling us to let justice roll down like waters.

In the name of Jesus we pray.

Amen

Beatitudes regarding Water: A Litany

(Suggestion: One voice for line one, two voices for line two, "all" for line three, and so on.)

Blessed are those who carry water up the hill on their heads.

Blessed too are the hands that dig a well so the children can go to school instead of to the distant water hole.

Blessed are the poor in spirit, for theirs is the kingdom of heaven.

Blessed are those whose gifts of bottled water are piled up in churches in Michigan.

Blessed too are those who raise their voices about the poison in their pipes and in their children.

Blessed are those who mourn, for they will be comforted.

Blessed are those who offer cups of water to marathon runners.

Blessed even are those who toss the water in the runners' faces!

Blessed are the meek, for they will inherit the earth.

Blessed are the children who spring joyously into the pool.

Blessed are the children who push wearily through the waves to drag in their fishnets.

Blessed are those who hunger and thirst for righteousness, for they will be filled.

Blessed are those who faithfully water the petunias the children will give away on Mother's Day.

Blessed too are the ones who faithfully water our children's spirits with their teaching.

Blessed are the merciful, for they will receive mercy.

Blessed are those who dribble water on the heads of sleeping babies, crying babies, laughing babies, and declare them all to belong to Jesus Christ.

Blessed also are those who immersed their whole selves in water to begin their new life in Christ.

Blessed are the pure in heart, for they will see God.

Blessed are those who jump in mud puddles with abandon.

Blessed also are those who go to court and to capitols to protest when those puddles are polluted.

Blessed are the peacemakers, for they will be called children of God.

⤞ ● ⤝

QUESTIONS FOR REFLECTION/ACTION

1. Think of a time when an encounter with water brought you joy or relief: plunging into the pool or the ocean, running in the water from the open fire hydrant or sprinkler, the first cold drink after exertion. Stay in that feeling for a moment; share a line of thanks to God about it if you wish.

2. What can we do in our daily use of water to protect this resource?

3. Think about a normal day in your life: what would happen, if you didn't have access to clean water on this one day?

4. Are there any initiatives working for clean water as a basic human right in my community? Are there any nearby that support such work in other parts of the world? If not, should/can we start one?

⤞ ● ⤝

Detlev Knoche was born in 1958 and is pastor of the Protestant Church in Hesse and Nassau (EKHN), director of the Ecumenical Center of EKHN and of the Evangelical Church of Kurhessen-Waldeck, and Ecumenical Liaison Officer of EKHN.

After careers in parish ministry and conference ministry, **Marian P. Shearer** is trying on retirement. Fortunately retired ministers get to preach, write prayers, and agitate for justice whenever we please.

41 LIVING RELATIONALLY IN A CULTURE OF ACQUISITIVENESS, A TIME OF DRAMATIC INEQUALITIES, AND A FRAGILE CREATION

Suggested Reading: Isaiah 55:1–3

What is needed to sustain life? Clean water, nutritious food, protective clothing, and sufficient shelter. What is needed to sustain life well? Space and time to imagine and search for meaning and purpose. As people who have dedicated time to exploring meaning and purpose within the Christian tradition, we wonder: How can we live well individually and communally?

Juggling two or three part-time jobs leaves many inadequate time for rest and relaxation. People work to meet basic needs, to sustain themselves and their families. They depend on a complex network of shared work and customer consumption.

Economic pressures force them to find alternative ways to meet basic needs. Individuals and communities pursue creative ways to grow food and share the cost of shelter. Some initiate, benefit from, and share urban gardens and communal housing. Resurgent interest in traditional handcrafts saves money and serves as personal and communal defiance. Relationships drive a new social and political activism, giving depth, meaning, and purpose to lives. While many aspects of this way of life are inspiring, how will those who depend on consumption and those who reject it collaborate to meet and sustain life for all?

Communities and congregations aware of the concerns and pressures of those in need can offer space and resources for collaborative spiritual conversation. A serious and playful approach invites exploration and experimentation in a safe, nonjudgmental environment. As we think of our neighbors, we ask:

Who is a part of our community? Are there interlocking communities?

What are their interests and needs?

What basic needs can our community respond to with the resources we have?

How is God inviting new relationships in our community?

How does the struggle to survive transform when it is shared?

PERSONAL PRAYER

We've walked with our children
down the toy aisle of the store
and watched them want everything in sight.
> So we bought them one thing, maybe two.
> Then we went home.

And we watched as our children discovered
they didn't really want what we just brought home.

We watched as they discovered again,
and we discovered with them,
what they really wanted—

> Grandpa, read me a story.
> Mommy, push me on the swing.
> Sister, come play catch with me.
> Brother, let us walk in the woods.
> Neighbor, will you play softball?
> Friend, do you know how to catch tadpoles?

Daddy, can I feel the whiskers of your beard?
Grandma, let's share cookies and tea.

Wise and generous God,
help us want what we really want!

Suggested Reading: Luke 12:22–23, from **The Message**

Jesus echoes the prophet Isaiah, raising the question: How do we become distracted and preoccupied by laboring for what does not satisfy us?

COMMUNITY PRAYER

Holy God, parent and child,
    we seek a new view.
Immersed in your presence,
    open us to our neighbors.
We admit that we don't know where to start
    and that our neighbor sometimes
    seems mysterious and unknowable.

Help us to see and appreciate diversity
    in our community.
Break our stubborn hearts.
    Open our minds to recognize the daily challenges of others.
Rather than provide answers
    or try to fix situations we may not understand,
    fill us with childlike curiosity so we can explore life together.

Bring an awareness of young voices into our lives.
    Renew in us the promise of possibilities.
And keep us honest, God.
Let our efforts be unsullied by ulterior motives like
    increased membership or maintenance of the status quo.

We seek new vision and renewed spirit
    for the pure joy of learning and being in relationship.
Amen

⤛ • ⤜

QUESTIONS FOR REFLECTION/ACTION

The verses from Isaiah 55 suggest human beings spend too much time pursuing things that do not sustain life. The words of Isaiah invite us to "come" and enjoy the good things, to "listen" to God and one another and live.

1. How much of the struggle to survive is solitary?
2. How much of the struggle to survive is communal?
3. How does the struggle to survive change when it becomes a shared struggle?
4. How can those who depend on consumption and those who reject it collaborate to meet and sustain life for all?

⤛ • ⤜

Dan Gansch-Boythe stocked shelves for a large retail chain store during the time of this writing. He holds a Bachelor's degree in Piano Performance, a Master of Divinity in Pastoral Studies and a Doctor of Ministry in Preaching—all of which prepared him well for his current role as sexton of the UCC church he and his spouse attend.

Kathryn C. Smith pastors a congregation near a large university. She is a parent of two college graduates in their mid-twenties. She is also related to and acquainted with young adults without this privilege. These young adults must learn to survive in an economic system devoted to limitless acquisition and consumption while discovering how to live well.

PACKING IT ALL IN
THE SOCIAL, ECONOMIC, AND ENVIRONMENTAL IMPACT OF TOURISM

42 ❋

The word "vacation" often fills us with a magnificent sense of excitement. No matter how much we may enjoy our daily lives, a break in routine, an opportunity to see new places, or a chance to rest and recuperate are part and parcel of a precious and limited resource. Vacation is not available to everyone, and for those who do not receive this gift, it may look vastly different.

For some, a single day off might be a yearned for release; others are fortunate enough to spend weeks or even months exploring, visiting old friends, or learning about new cultures. It's impossible to deny the pleasure of these excursions, just as it's impossible to deny the profound effect tourism has on poverty-stricken regions. While we may strive to be socially responsible in our day-to-day lives, it's easy to forget, when traveling to another city or country, that our pleasure may come at another's cost.

Tourism, especially in many developing countries, is a considerable piece of the economic puzzle. As visiting remote and rural locations becomes increasingly popular, we have to consider the impact we have when we choose to travel someplace new. Are we spending money with companies who treat employees in a just manner? Are we aware of any damage our presence has on the existing culture, people, and environment? Are we choosing to feed our own curiosity at the "invisible" expense of others? Are we courteous visitors?

Traveling is an incredible gift. It is also a responsibility. When we drive, fly, hike, or boat away from home, we must remember to open ourselves to the truth around us. How are we using our privilege to improve the lives of others? How can we support the cultures we visit? How do we protect the earth for generations to come? Vacation, sabbatical, holiday— we all seek renewal, regardless of its availability, in our own ways. May we choose to do so with the same compassion, gentleness, and understanding we strive for in our daily work.

PERSONAL PRAYER

Gentle spirit, we ask that you sit with us on this train.
Hold tight to our hearts and tongues as we fly across the world
or travel down highways and across state lines.
We ask that you grant us patience with the journey,
with the people who collect our tolls, carry our luggage,
guide us down new roads. We ask that you open our hearts
not just to novel experiences, but to how this trip might have a lasting effect
on the people we meet or the paths we stumble down.

We ask that you remind us, God—remind us in your tender
persistent whisper—to look at the faces around us,
to consider the person we rent this car from, the family we learn to cook
exotic new foods with, the animals who are captured and kept
for our entertainment. Remind us, holy one, of the invisible hands
cleaning our rooms, the forgettable faces serving us dinner, the children
begging in the streets of whom we have been "warned."

God keep this message alive in our hearts—
that people are not art, people are not a photograph
flashed and then forgotten, people are not a day's worth
of lessons about what it means to be poor.

Your people, God—all people—are born precious
in your sight. Your people are born strong and different
and beautiful, a reflection of this magnificent planet with its
tundra and peaks, beaches, deep forests, and dark canyons.
Your people are born with the right to live unmolested,
to share their lives as they choose instead of as others demand.
Your people have a right to Sabbath, to a rest from prying, curious,
even loving hearts. God, remind us to step gently, to embrace
　　　that enthusiasm
to learn something new, and to be sure we're always, always speaking
and searching and resting in your light.
Amen

COMMUNITY PRAYER

ONE: God, we ask forgiveness for the many times we have sought
pleasure at the expense of our brothers and sisters.

MANY: **God, we give thanks for the new people we meet, for the
stories shared, for the communities built when we travel away from
home and our own comfort zone.**

ONE: God, we ask forgiveness for the carbon emissions we haven't
considered, for the tanks of gasoline burned, and for the roads cut
where once there were none as we seek a glimpse of your face in once
remote and untouched wilderness.

MANY: **God, we give thanks for the sun we have seen set over new
horizons, for the serenity of the mountains we've scaled, for the glory
of tiny islands nestled in deep blue seas.**

ONE: God, we ask forgiveness for pushing down our own doubts as to
where our tourist dollars have gone, who is benefitting, and how we
might be enslaving others in our pursuit of novel experiences.

MANY: **God, we give thanks for your constant prompting, for your
reminder that we can do better, that we can care more deeply and
work harder—even in the midst of a holiday—to love your people
as we are loved.**

ALL: Give thanks that ours is a God of seeking, of questioning and exploring; a God of love, all-knowing and merciful in the face of careless acts as well as atrocity; a God of industry, constantly working within us to make waves of change for the better. Let us hear the whisper of God's word within and turn each new encounter into an opportunity to create a safe and beautiful Sabbath for all people. Amen

→→ • ←←

QUESTIONS FOR REFLECTION/ACTION

1. How much do we know about the effects of tourism on the poorest communities in the places we travel?

2. How much research have we done before we travel to determine that the services we are using, to the best of our abilities, are in line with our desire for just, compassionate treatment of people and the environment?

3. Have we considered what impact we have on the communities we visit? Socially? Economically? Environmentally?

→→ • ←←

Maria Mankin has published five resource books with Pilgrim Press, as well as contributed to several poetry and essay anthologies. She writes a weekly literary review, Books J'adore (booksjadore.com), with an audience of twenty-five thousand and recently published *Circ*, a collaborative novel with Pigeon Park Press. She is currently working on a second novel as well as a children's book.

4 3 ✳ WASTE

Waste made by humans is continuing to grow exponentially through-out the world, putting great strain on the environment. Yet those who make the most waste are not likely to have to see it. Moreover, well-to-do communities often oppose attempts to create waste-to-energy plants or landfills nearby—a reaction that sometimes is called NIMBY (not in my backyard). Instead, the rubbish often ends up in the poor communities or regions of the world.

PERSONAL PRAYER

SHOPPING PLANS

Temptation can be
Stronger than the fear of the future
Stronger than the knowledge of the dangers
Stronger than the shame for what we are doing to our world.

And so I buy these things again and again:
Something I will use once
(If at all)
Something that didn't cost me much
But will cost the earth much more,

Adding to the ever growing mountain
Of waste,
Endangering those poorer than myself,
Poisoning the oceans,
Burdening the earth.

Loving, creating God,
Forgive me and help me recognize
Those moments of temptation.
Help me stop and think
Before I want,
Before I buy,
Before I waste.

As I look around
My home,
Help me to take joy
In simple things
And see how I could
Bring new life
To what would otherwise
Be considered worthless
And discarded.

COMMUNITY PRAYER

Prayer of Confession

Creating God,
We praise you and bless you,
For you make no waste.

All that you make is good.
There are no wasteful leftovers of your labor.
Everything has a purpose.

Yet we are so quick to make waste—
Mountains and mountains of it.

Waste around us,
Waste sent far away from us,
Waste inside us;
Waste of time,
Waste of effort,
Waste of resources.

So help us, Creating God,
To learn to live
Less wastefully.

Take us to your workshop
And teach us
The aptitude for saving,
The skill of repurposing,
The art of renewing.

↠ • ↞

QUESTIONS FOR REFLECTION/ACTION

1. Try to recall all the things you have thrown away this week—at home, into trash bins on the street, or at your workplace. Put it all mentally together in one pile. How big is the pile? It may be good to take up an exercise of writing down for a day or a whole week everything you are throwing away.

2. Can you identify the settings in which you are most tempted to buy something that will result in unnecessary waste? How could you recognize those settings in a way that would prompt you to pause and perhaps decide not to increase waste?

3. What kind of waste could you (personally or communally) turn into something useful, and how?

4. Do you recognize what kinds of waste are hazardous in the particular sense of "household or industrial hazardous waste" and what kinds of waste by its amount are dangerous to ocean

creatures, to human beings, to vegetation, to drinking water? Can you become involved in advocacy?

→⊱ • ⊰←

Born in Lithuania, **Lina Toth (Andronoviene)** is assistant principal and lecturer at the Scottish Baptist College situated in Paisley, near Glasgow. A musician and artist as well as a theologian, she is particularly interested in exploring various aspects of ethics, spirituality, and theology of culture.

I am often caught by what children need in order to laugh. They need enough: enough nutrition, enough mentoring, enough education, enough safety, enough love. Children who live amid abundance and children who live in the wake of disaster and ongoing crises need the same things. Our commitment must be to stay the course in ongoing compassion rather than simply arriving with the emergency resources and disappearing again.

PERSONAL PRAYER

God of Love and of joy and laughter, we celebrate each and every time a child is free to laugh; laugh at the world, laugh at those who love and teach, laugh at the miracle of a smile and an outstretched hand.

We celebrate Zeinab, nine going on two, because of a neurological disorder, as she climbs into her exhausted and agitated mother's lap, looks deep into her eyes, and busts up laughing. We laugh at the laughter and tickle fight that follows.

God of the outstretched hand, we celebrate the laughter of fourteen-year-old Donzi, living on a mountain in earthquake ravaged Haiti as he sees his name written out for the first time.

God of delightful silliness, we celebrate, too, a tall, blond twenty-eight-year-old adult playing gana gana goose with the laughing children of a small isolated coastal village in Haiti.

God of the open heart, we celebrate the laughter of Ahmed as he skips through a Mosque that used to be a church, safe to learn about Allah at a time when Allah is an enemy to so many around him.

God of unbridled and persistent hope, we celebrate the laughter of young girls playing double-dutch jump rope on a sweltering street in a city in New York.

God of joy, we celebrate the laughter as a two-year-old tries to wink back at the pastor who just winked at him.

Creator God, we celebrate the laughter of young children and young-at-heart adults playing in the ocean.

God of each and every smile, of each and every chuckle, join your laughter to ours as we work diligently to help more children laugh.

COMMUNITY PRAYER

ONE: A child laughs when that child has enough: enough food, enough shelter, enough clothing.

MANY: **Grant us wisdom, O God, enough to provide adequate food shelter and clothing to all of the children throughout the earth.**

ONE: A child laughs when she has access to opportunities to learn, to grow in mind and spirit.

MANY: **Grant us strength enough, O God, to step up and fight for the resources to ensure all children have the chance to learn and grow and develop self- confidence.**

ONE: A child laughs when he is valued just as he is, is celebrated just as he is.

MANY: **Grant us humility, O God, to delight in all children no matter their gender, their race, their weight, their economic status, their faith, their gender identity, or their abilities.**

ONE: A child laughs when that child feels safe.

MANY: Grant us courage, O God, to create cities and countryside safe for all children, and to create sanctuaries for children living in dangerous environments.

ONE: A child laughs when she has adults to affirm and encourage her growth and development.

MANY: Help us find the time, O God, to be that adult.

ALL: We laugh, God, when children laugh. And you, too, too burst forth with a great big delightful belly laugh when children laugh. Let us hear the children's laughter joined with yours.

→> • <←

QUESTIONS FOR REFLECTION/ACTION

1. Notice the children in your family, neighborhood, city, or town. Do they seem happy? Free? What needs are lacking in their lives? Full funding for their schools? A group of people to ensure their safety? Enough food to eat? Adults willing to be present in their lives? Write down five needs. Choose two. Write down three things you can do to begin to address those needs.

2. Now do the same exercise for children in settings covered by today's news. What are their needs and how will they receive them? Can you be a part of that change?

3. Finally, think about what was newsworthy a year ago or two years ago. Is help still reaching these families? Is your faith community or denomination a part of that assistance? Compare the results of your three questions.

→> • <←

Terri McNamara serves a small church in Philadelphia, Pennsylvania. She has a passion for mission and working on the margins.

45 ✳ SPECIES PROTECTION IN THE MIDST OF MASS EXTINCTION

Achipmunk dashes out of the stone wall in my backyard and tumbles over her sibling in an epic race for an acorn. I giggle from my tree-limb front-row seat. An earthworm squirms to the surface as my mother's hands work garden soil. Its industrious wiggle makes me smile. A catfish jumps and startles a dignified goose. My dad and I laugh at their antics from our rest stop off the bike trail. As a child, few things brought me more joy than these moments. I didn't need a Sunday school lesson to know why. Then and now, I feel deeply that these are the times I am closest to my Creator. Every expression of God's creation reveals something unique to me about the Divine.

I want children everywhere, now and into the future, to feel the joy of dwelling among a diversity of wild creatures. To protect these experiences for future generations, we need to take hope-filled action now. Right now, our planet is in the midst of the greatest species loss it has experienced since the dinosaurs went extinct. One in five species is threatened or endangered.

Action to protect God's creatures from extinction is not altruism. It is about protecting the integrity of the web of creation, which enables *all of us* to thrive. When we care for the native plants, insects, fish, birds, and animals in our own ecosystem, we care for ourselves. Like the system of the body in 1 Corinthians 12, we are interdependent. When one suffers, we all suffer.

In July 2016, *Science* magazine featured a study showing that in more than half of the world's landmass, habitat destruction has caused unsafe levels of decline in plant and animal biodiversity. The study goes on to explain that agriculture and human health are at risk in many of these areas. The fate of humans and of animals are bound up together.

It is time for a shift in the way we perceive our human role in God's creation. Consider one reading of Genesis, which Rev. Dr. Curt Karns of the Presbyterian Church (USA) in Alaska learned with the Yupik peoples in southwest Alaska. For the Yupik, and for many Native cultures, it is a core value to honor elders and ancestors. They noticed that Genesis 2:4 says "These are the generations of the heavens and the earth when they were created," and that everywhere else in the Bible that says "these are the generations of . . . " has a genealogy attached to it. What if we were to reread Genesis as if the skies, the waters, the land, plants, and all God's creatures were our elders in creation, deserving of our utmost respect and care?

PERSONAL PRAYER

Evening Prayer of Gratitude for God's Creatures

God, thank you for all the ways your creatures ministered to me today.

For the fruits and vegetables I ate, I thank the bees, butterflies, and bats that pollinated them.

For the air I breathed, I thank the trees that cycled carbon dioxide into oxygen, as well as the birds and woodland creatures that carry and bury trees' seeds to help them multiply and thrive.

For the water I used to quench my thirst and bathe, to wash dishes and clothes, I thank the fish and other creatures for sharing it with me.

For sounds that filled my day: buzzing, chirping, purring, barking, scurrying—I thank a diversity of creatures for reminding me I am not alone.

God of all creatures, I am grateful every day for your web of creation.

Out of that gratitude flows my desire to cherish, protect, restore, and rightly share our common earthly home.
Amen

COMMUNITY PRAYER

Organize a Creature-Counting Activity or "BioBlitz" for your Community

Conditions for God's creatures are changing fast, and it is difficult for all of us to monitor and address these changes. Taking a group to spend twenty minutes or more to engage in creature-counting and observation can make us more mindful and observant of God's web of creation. It can also make us citizen scientists who help professionals such as watershed stewardship organizations and land management agencies with data collection. Groups can count and observe creatures on church grounds, a community center, a retreat center, or a local park. In the United States, the National Park Service and National Geographic offer resources on their websites to help your community to engage in a what they call a "BioBlitz."

Prayer for Creature-Counting and Observation

Creator God, thank you for making us one of a diversity of creatures in your web of creation. Thank you for entrusting this web of creation to our care. Open our eyes to the ways all your creation reveals truths about you, our Creator. Open our minds to new insights from your creatures' gifts—how they solve problems, build community, and embrace their creature-hood. Open our hearts to cherish, protect, restore, and rightly share our common home.

→> • <←

QUESTIONS FOR REFLECTION/ACTION

1. What are the plants and animals I most interact with, and how do they influence my understanding of who I am in the family of creation?

2. Is my connection to the web of creation nourishing my prayer life? My personal life? My career choices? My political engagement?

3. How does my lifestyle impact my fellow creatures? (For example, does my garden include native plants that can nourish pollinators? Do I avoid pesticides? To what extent do my food choices create demand for habitat destruction?)

→ • ←

Shantha Ready Alonso is the executive director of Creation Justice Ministries, an ecumenical organization that equips, educates, and mobilizes Christian communities to protect, restore, and rightly share God's creation. She is active at St. Camillus multicultural Franciscan parish in Silver Spring, Maryland.

46 ✳ RHYTHM AND BALANCE
LIVING IN AN OVER-STRESSED WORLD

One of our biggest contemporary problems is a number of smaller concerns broadly lumped together under the term "burnout." I hear "burnout" applied to clergy, to doctors, to social workers, to people in just about every walk of life. Now I am hearing it applied to children.

It reminds me of a time, many years ago, when I was a music teacher. Two little girls—sisters—came each week for their lesson. I would work with one while the other sat on my couch, sometimes reading, sometimes just sitting. One day, one of the girls was reading an article in a magazine about overscheduled children, which complained that children did not have time to play, to sit under a tree, to be children. She said, "This could be me and my sister."

This could be said of many children. I see them playing hockey, taking music lessons, going to gymnastics, skiing, tutoring after school—the list goes on. Their weekends are taken up with tournaments; they are doing schoolwork in between other activities; they are moving all the time. Even as we are striving for balance in our own lives, let us not forget the children. There is nothing wrong with children having time for themselves; there is nothing wrong with children being bored; there is nothing wrong with children doing a little precious nothing.

PERSONAL PRAYER

Creator God, I pray for the children—
the children who skate
the children who dance
the children who sing
the children who are busy
every day of the week.

I pray that somewhere,
sometime, somehow
they will be given grace
the grace to rest in your love
the grace to gaze at the stars
the grace to listen to a birdsong.

I pray for the parents
so that they will see
how important it is
for their children
not to be scheduled
all day, every day.

I pray that parents and children
will find the time to be together
to share a snack—cookies and milk—
to read a book, to watch a movie,
to talk, to laugh, to cry, to cuddle,
just to be.

Help us, God, as adults,
to be available for our children
and for other children
to recognize them as precious

as gifts from you
to be cherished.
Amen

COMMUNITY PRAYER

LEADER: God, we are grateful for our children. Help us to remember that they are only ours for a little while, and that our biggest job is to prepare them to leave us.

PEOPLE: **May we guard our children and keep them from harm.**

LEADER: Each child has special abilities. Help us to recognize these abilities and encourage our children to develop them as you would wish.

PEOPLE: **May we watch over our children as they grow and find their skills. May we encourage them but, at the same time, allow them to choose what they want to do.**

LEADER: Each child will face challenges. Help us to see these challenges not as obstacles, but rather as a means of discovering new ways of living life.

PEOPLE: **May we allow our children to fail sometimes, and teach them that true failure lies in giving up.**

LEADER: Each child needs faith. Help us to bring them up with faith— faith in themselves, faith in us, and, most of all, faith in you.

PEOPLE: **May we teach our children to pray. May we show them that prayer is a part of our daily life so that, as they grow, it will be a part of theirs.**

LEADER: Each child needs structure, but they also need freedom. Help us to teach them how to find a balance between the two.

PEOPLE: **May we show our children a balanced life by making sure that our own lives are also balanced, with a good mix of work and play.**

LEADER: Each child needs love. Help us to show them the love that you show us, forgiving them when they need it, while at the same time letting them know that some behaviours are not acceptable.

PEOPLE: May we love our children. May we live lives of love, modeling what true love looks like so that they will recognize it in themselves.

LEADER: Each child needs boundaries. Help us to help them learn how to set their own boundaries—physical boundaries, emotional boundaries —so that they will be able to protect themselves, in every sense of the word.

PEOPLE: May we model boundary-setting for our children. May we show them that there are always people who will try to cross boundaries and give them the courage to stand up for themselves.

LEADER: Each child needs adults who care. Help us to be those adults for however many children come into our lives, whether we are the parents or not.

PEOPLE: May we remember that children are the most vulnerable of all. May we make it our mission never to place them in harm's way, and, if they are already there, may we do what needs to be done to remove them from it.

ALL: Lord, we thank you for all of the children. We ask that you be with us as we guide them into a future that we can only imagine. We ask that you be with them so that, as time goes on, they, too, will grow into the adults you always intended them to be. We ask that, no matter what comes into their lives, there will always be time for them to sit with you, time for them not to be busy, time for them just to be. Amen

⤜ • ⤛

QUESTIONS FOR REFLECTION/ACTION

1. What fears cause parents to overbook children—fear of recreational drugs and alcohol, fear of difficult friends, fear of having a "short" portfolio, fear of not being able to boast in front of other parents?

2. What steps can you, if you are a parent, take to ensure that your child is not overbooked? How can you persuade them that downtime is even more necessary than busy time?

3. How can you model a healthy balance in your own life for your child?

4. Have you ever considered scheduling downtime? For some people, especially people living in the twenty-first century, the only way to make sure that something happens is to put it into an agenda. Discuss whether or not this would work for you and the children in your life.

➤➤ • ◄◄

Katherine Burgess is the minister at St. Andrew's Presbyterian Church in Quebec City. Prior to ministry, she taught French, Music, and English Language and Literature. As a minister, she's a teacher, but with a different focus. She lives in a beautiful walled city with her husband, Keith, and large dog, Bella.

47 ✳ EQUAL ACCESS TO TECHNOLOGY AND INTERNET

If you could see me writing these words, you would see me in an environment and with technological tools that are typical given my age, gender, economic status, and geography. I am writing on an Apple laptop in a Starbucks franchise near the heart of Silicon Valley. However, that does not capture the full background of this social location: this particular Starbucks is in the city of East Palo Alto, a beautifully diverse yet economically distressed community of about 2.5 square miles, largely bypassed by the affluence and innovation surrounding it.

It seems strange, in this country, and especially in this particular valley, to be discussing disparities in basic access to the Internet and its resources. For many people in this region, high-speed broadband Internet access at home is a given—I would go so far as to say for a very large segment of the population, it ranks next to safe water and reliable electricity as a hallmark individual housing right in our modern society.

Yet home Internet service can be a challenge here—the poor infrastructure combined with lack of interest for reinvestment by the corporate service providers results in slow speeds and zero competition in most residential areas. One single provider is the only option for broadband in the majority of the city. In the meantime, East Palo Alto is home to the last remaining tract of affordable housing along the San Francisco Peninsula, with more than 50 percent of all identified low- and middle-income housing units in this region contained within these 2.5 square miles.

While tech companies, both established and startup, seek to disrupt industries, sectors, and processes, their offices are cleaned and their legendary gourmet employee meals are served in large part by residents of this local community. Shuttle drivers, shoppers and couriers for on-demand delivery services, and car-sharing drivers are disproportionately East Palo Alto denizens. Even as those same companies create new platforms for education and learning, the local elementary school district here remains a basic-aid district resembling a different universe from its surrounding districts.

And yet, as I look around this Starbucks, I see hope. I see what this community has to offer the others surrounding it. There are plenty of laptops and "iDevices," mobile phones and tablets. Across them, people are talking and sharing. Two children are reading an interactive book with an adult on an iPad in the corner. A woman is meeting with a high school teenager crouched over a shared laptop looking at college websites. A group of young men are playing a multiplayer game at the opposite end of that table, laughing and egging each other on. And across from me a young woman is also working on a personal project—we've kept an eye on each other's computers when we've had to take phone calls outside or head back to the counter for refills.

Our local library has a similar sight. People are not there simply taking advantage of the access to technology in order to search and apply for jobs, to communicate with family and friends in other parts of the country or world, or to learn new skills through online training programs. They talk with their neighbors, engage in a bit of career networking, and check in on each other.

That's when I realize the question has been framed wrong all along. Here, in these hidden parts of our United States affluence, in a pocket of the most innovative region in human history, our technological access ought not be looked at as a divide or a deficiency in need of correction. Perhaps we should be asking why technology access has been cast as a commodity for the single individual in the first place.

PERSONAL PRAYER

God of community, of connection, of learning: I give you thanks for all the tools that make that possible. From simple conversation over a cup of coffee or tea to complex arrangements that make it possible for me to Skype with family and friends all around the world straight from my living room, the wonder of technology amazes me, and yet I wish that it were as easily accessible, integrated, and reliable in the more hidden parts as it is in the center of society. When I find myself immersed behind glowing electrons and more comfortable communicating through touchscreens and keyboards, remind me to lift up my head and embrace the world you love.

Alleluia and amen

COMMUNITY PRAYER

A Call to Confession and Reflection

ONE: In the hidden places and the public spaces,

ALL: **We stumble as we play Pokemon Go on our phones.**

ONE: When God pokes and the Holy Spirit calls,

ALL: **We poke back on Facebook, and we ignore the message on voicemail.**

ONE: For those times when our neighbor is asking for help right in front of us,

ALL: **And we say, "Send me an e-mail so I can get to you later,"**

ONE: When we get upset at our slow Internet connection,

ALL: **Because our Netflix binge session is buffering,**

ONE: And we fail to consider the human suffering involved in mining Rare Earth elements required to power all of this technology,

ALL: **Forgive us, O God.**

ONE: When our personal satisfaction becomes an obstacle for doing our work in Christlike liberation,

ALL: **Show us your face, O God.**

ONE: When the ease, comfort, and simplicity of mediated community appeals more than the hard work of building your Beloved Community,

ALL: **Lift up our heads and hands, O God.**

→→ • ←←

QUESTIONS FOR REFLECTION/ACTION

1. Technology is so multifaceted—tools for connection, platforms for entertainment, various means of commerce and education. From the light bulb to the handheld computer, consider all the ways in which you significantly engage with modern technology.

2. If you have reliable broadband access at home, what would it be like if you had to rely on publicly available wi-fi or public computers instead? How would that change the way you engage with technology? And if you rely on publicly available wi-fi or public computers, how do you think having broadband access at home would change the way you engage with technology?

3. Some of the most hidden and egregious environmental and human rights violations are occurring in relationship to electronics manufacture and operation. Will you research these issues and make a commitment to speak out on behalf of oppressed communities to businesses that profit from this continued cycle of destruction?

→→ • ←←

Daniel Ross-Jones is Associate Conference Minister for the Northern California Northern Nevada Conference of the United Church of Christ. He loves gadgets, road trips, mountains, the ocean, and donuts—particularly of the jelly-filled variety.

ON BEING OUTSIDE
OF THE NORMS

48 ACCEPTING A SPECTRUM OF
BEHAVIORS ON THE JOURNEY
AND AS A JOURNEY

There is a child who can be counted on to be boisterous, especially during the quiet parts of a worship service. Sliding the length of the hardwood floors of the church sanctuary on his belly underneath the pews, or walking back and forth on a front pew as if he were a gymnast on a balance beam, he expresses himself with constant movement. Adults tend to define his behavior as a problem and as falling outside of acceptable norms, but if it is indeed a problem, why does he look so joyful as he slides, wiggles, whirls, runs, and jumps?

This reflection is offered on behalf of all those children in our midst who seem, in increasing numbers, to be labeled "hyperactive" and to be diagnosed with attention deficit disorder (ADD). As a minister currently blessed with three such kinetically inclined young parishioners, and a mother who has struggled to honor, direct, and channel the formidable energies of two sons with ADD over the years, I am deeply familiar with the daily challenges and joys of raising such children.

Creativity and *joie de vivre* are two of their charms, yet all too often they are labeled, marginalized, medicated, blamed, and shamed in ways that threaten their personhood. Many an artist and gifted leader has emerged when such a child grows into an ability to harness the blessings of boundless energy, sensitivity to noticing many things at once, and the ability to focus intensely on their particular interests.

PERSONAL PRAYER

O GOD, MY CHILD CAN'T SIT STILL

See, O God of the Whirlwind, my child's exuberance! See how she moves, animated by an inner energy that delights like a fresh breeze, a breeze infused with laughter! Loving movement for its own sake, she bounces, runs, twirls, slides, and jumps. Her joy bubbles over—it is built right in. How fully she loves life! How well she knows that which satisfies her soul! And yet, O God, so often, she does not fit in. So often, she is seen as problematic.

Help me, O God who parents. Grant me the wisdom, energy, and grace to keep a step ahead of my child, and to help order his world in a way that allows him to safely express his true self.

Show me, O God who reveals. Show me the way to teach my child to learn from consequences, to manage his impulsivity, and to take the measure of a situation before jumping; help me offer these crucial life lessons without an inference that my child is "bad."

Calm me, O God who soothes. Help me keep my cool when my child can't contain herself, especially in public. Aid me in balancing the roles of being my child's ambassador, defender, and teacher. When I can't tell if she truly is to blame for the latest classroom catastrophe, help me to ask the right questions. Help me hold her accountable at the right times, and to deconstruct the tendency to find her guilty at those times she is unfairly blamed.

Bless my child, my friend's child, my church's child, my community's child, O God. May their bounce survive all the push-back, and may their energy be harnessed in a thousand good and wonderful ways. Thank you for their sparkle, their spirit, and their specialness.

Amen

COMMUNITY PRAYER

Responsive Prayer for Adults Seeking to Build Intergenerational Community

(This prayer is written for the church setting, but can be adapted for other settings, such as schools, family gatherings, etc.)

ONE: There is Tim again, sliding on his belly under the pews, from the front of the church to the back.

MANY: **Help us, O God, to guide Tim with care rather than to criticize his parents.**

ONE: There is Libby again, running by the lit candles, nearly toppling one over.

MANY: **Help us, O God, to be part of the village that raises Libby, rather than rolling our eyes from a distance.**

ONE: There is Thomas again, talking out loud through all the opening prayers.

MANY: **Help us, O God, to find a way to include in our prayers those words that come out of the mouths of babes.**

ONE: There is Sherrie again, throwing a tantrum on the floor.

MANY: **Help us, O God, to offer Sherrie's mom a helping hand.**

ONE: There is Luke again, running through the crowd, nearly knocking over some of the elders.

MANY: **Help us, O God, to show Luke why it's important to walk sometimes rather than to run, and to give him a job that he can be proud to do at such times.**

ONE: There is Ella again, drawing on the pews.

MANY: **Help us, O God, to give Ella a place to make her art.**

ALL: Gracious God, build among us a community that makes, holds, and maintains functional, purposeful, and carefully thought-out space and spaces for our children. Give us the joy of living with loving intention as an intergenerational community. Amen

→→ • ←←

QUESTIONS FOR REFLECTION/ACTION

1. How can we best involve and engage very physically active children in our public spaces?

2. When is discipline important, and what does constructive discipline look like? Can the word return to "disciple" or has it been taken over by negativism and we need to find a new word?

3. How can community members constructively take part in being supportive to the parents of children who are impulsive and very active?

→→ • ←←

Mary A. James is the mom of three adult children of various delightful temperaments, ranging from that of kinetic dreamer to effervescent calm. Both temperaments have found expression in her grandchildren as well. She is also a pastor, currently serving at First Congregational Church of Wakefield, New Hampshire, a loving open and affirming congregation.

49 ✳ THE WONDER OF DISCOVERY
ENCOURAGING THE EVOLUTION OF EDUCATION

Education allows us to expand, to grow beyond the barriers of our body, our social condition, our time. . . . It allows for forward motion . . . continuation . . . discovery . . . wonder . . .

Where does learning happen? Everywhere. With people, with nature, with God. How does learning happen? By listening. Watching. Interacting. Experimenting.

Why does learning happen? It's integral to who we are as humans, as the beloved of God, as co-creators with God.

For some education is a privilege or a dream, while for others it is an expectation. For some an educational experience may be frustrating and filled with barriers, while for others it may be an opening of windows. Education must be an affirmation of the diverse ways people learn. The need around the world is to make the environment for education nurturing, safe, affirming, holistic, and transforming of individuals and society.

PERSONAL PRAYER

Imagine a place or time where and when your heart and mind were open and you were able to learn something new that has made a difference in your life. Dwell in that place as you take time to imagine all the people who have no such place . . . all those who find themselves shut down or shut out from their natural inclination to thrive. As you pray these words, hold these eager children in your heart and in your mind.

To listen, O God. To react. To touch. To feel. To wonder. Each new moment . . . each new encounter . . . is an opportunity to learn. How wonderful that you surround us with so much and so many to encounter. How amazing and how affirming that you bless us with the ability to explore, analyze, and understand.

O God, for all the world around us and all you give us to learn, we thank you.

For our companions along the way . . . each of us differently abled, each of us unique in our understandings and curiosities . . .

For all the ways we help each other learn, grow, become.

For those who specialize in the art and science of teaching . . . who dedicate their lives and answer your call to nurture others even in circumstances less than ideal, we thank you.

And for our children who even in the bleakest times and places manage to find the joy, to discover the light, to grow and gather and make their way into learning . . . we thank you.

For all of us, your learners of this world, we pray that the vast knowledge of life be written in our hearts and in our lives, that we may find our way while finding you imprinted on every text, in every raindrop and within the spirits of all your peoples.

God who knows we will never understand everything, we pray we accept no limits to what is possible with and for you.

So we pray for safe havens of learning.

We pray for our children, that every child in every place may live and grow and blossom into the wonder you intended.

We pray for cooperation and the dedication of our leaders and decision makers to decide first for education.

We pray that together we may all strive for a world where all people may creatively respond to you from the depths of their hearts . . . writing, painting, reading, singing, composing, dancing, experimenting, praying, organizing, and celebrating all of this, all of you, all that is this wonder we know as life.

O God we pray it so.

COMMUNITY PRAYER

A Responsive Reading for Growth

Creator of the stars and moon, you beckon us with your lights to reach and to dream.

You tease and entice us to reach for the sky. You help us believe it is within our grasp.

Weaver of the fields and meadows, you move us with a gentle breeze, nurturing our curiosity.

You show us layers of life that surround us, the tall grass above and the tiny ants below.

Painter of the sunrises and sunsets, you quiet us with your beauty.

You create space within us for awe and amazement, for humility and gratitude.

Goddess of the ocean, you teach us balance: when to push and when to pull.

We learn there is a time for giving and a time for receiving; a time for learning and a time for teaching. And all take part in the cycle.

You who dance to the rhythm of the river,

We experience different currents throughout our life, sometimes a slow steady trickle, sometimes a raging rapid, and sometimes a full stop at a beaver's home.

The world is our classroom. The moments for learning something new are endless.

We give thanks for the ability to grow, to change, and to evolve. Our hearts learn to expand and to explore. Thank you, Great Teacher and Great Student, for the many ways to grow beyond our edges, for the constant stream of love and support from you, and for the cycle that promises new life with every meeting.

A PRAYER FOR EDUCATION

Confession

God,
some say, "Knowledge is power," but we know this is not so without the tools, the budget, and enough qualified, dedicated teachers to guide our children to the knowledge they need to find their way in this world.

God,
we confess our failure to provide safe and nurturing places for all children. We confess many schools are not safe. Rooms are too small and in disrepair. Military budgets drain our resources and we chip away at public school budgets in favor of private schools, cheating those most in need of a good public education.

God who gave us the one so often called Teacher,
forgive us all the ways we fail to support our teachers with the income, time, and trust they need. And forgive us for favoring some children while leaving behind others because of their race, their class, their gender, their sexual orientation, or learning style.

Forgive us all the ways we tell ourselves someone else will fix this. Guide us through that dark hole of denial to the open road of freedom, change, empowerment, hope.

Trusting in your grace we pray
Amen

Assurance of Grace

God's school is love and God's curriculum is the place where hope and justice meet. We are taught that we can make a difference.

→➤ • ◄←

QUESTIONS FOR REFLECTION/ACTION

1. What is education?

2. What are the values of institutionalizing education and what are the limitations when education is institutionalized?

3. Name one lesson in an educational context that transformed your understanding and helped you become who you are now.

→➤ • ◄←

H. Rebecca Lockwood is the associate pastor of Mission and Education at St. Peter's UCC in Carmel, Indiana. Becca grew up in Maine and fell in love with the outdoors. She makes ceramics in her spare time, which allows her to create and play. Arguably one of the biggest Harry Potter fans, she reads the series every summer.

Diane E. Lockwood Wendorf, minister and artist, has served parishes in Ohio, Kentucky, Illinois, and Maine. Children, their education, ministry, creativity, leadership, and unabashed faithfulness has been the heart and help of her ministry. Diane currently serves North Parish UCC in Sanford, Maine.

50 PROTECTING A CHILD'S SENSE OF SELF IN A FAST-CHANGING WORLD

Is there a future of stability for children whose parents are refugees living in settlement camps? Can black children live lives unscathed by repeated exposure to police violence? Can youngsters and teens whose parents work long hours and barely make ends meet know that a brighter vocational future awaits them?

In response to injustice and loss of hope inflicting the world's children, Judaism, Christianity, and Islam unequivocally affirm God's undivided regard and tenderness for the most vulnerable. Indeed, the integrity, durability, and continuity of these religions declare that God's mercy, compassion, and love is without equal when it comes to children. Thus, as people of faith, we cannot do anything less than ensure that the collective future of all children be built upon responsible and just relationships.

Affirming that God unambiguously calls upon us to safeguard children from harm and provide them with life-giving opportunities, let us dedicate ourselves to ensuring that no child is exempt from being a valued and beloved son or daughter of the Most High. Let us seek just and sustainable circumstances across this planet so that all the world's children may savor childhood, free from harm's way. Let us declare that God's realm will only be realized when the vanguards of hope and justice include each and every child.

PERSONAL PRAYER

This could be the prayer of an aunt or uncle, a grandparent or godparent. Use any pronoun—he, she, xe, they. Because this is the personal prayer section, I am thinking about my grandson (Gayle). In our era of blended families, people often become "relatives" of children at different times and hope to have a rewarding relationship and succeed in being appropriate and responsive to parents' wishes. The final paragraph of this prayer may well be the beginning or base of just such a prayer.

Gracious God who has given us more than we deserve, and loving God who begins life in an act of love, my heart is swollen with hope on this day. This child with perfect fingers and toes also has a perfect future in front of him. Mistakes have not yet been made, selfishness not yet manifest, but we know they are coming, and we pray that you will remain by this child's side even in the hurt, disappointment, and failure ahead.

For you, O God, are the source of true worth for this child. Walk with him wherever his legs take you. In his life provide him with the opportunities he needs: to help bear disappointments and disasters and still experience success and joy; the opportunities to know love so that he may show love; the opportunities to experience peace wherever he goes; the opportunities to be rooted in You, so that the winds of change and challenge will not buffet him about.

And find a way for me to also be with this child, as support, as love, as grandma, so that together we are a team for this baby. May I be worthy to be a model for him when he is questioning. May I support his parents that they will nurture him. May I develop a relationship that is of value to us both.

Thank you for all of this, I pray in the name of Jesus Christ. Amen

COMMUNITY PRAYER

A Litany for Confirmation Sunday

This litany may be used in a service or it may be shared in a group meeting. Encourage members of the group to choose one of the metaphors as personally apt or create new metaphors for a formal prayer, which is then partially written by the group.

LEADER: Jesus described the realm of God as a realm where just and compassionate relationships are not only spoken of but also actively lived out. Jesus emphasized that the realm of God lies within you. Think of it! No matter who you are, where you've come from or where you're headed—God's realm is actively at work within you. Such that when you act with compassion and courage, when your words radiate advocacy and illuminate hope's justice, others see evidence of God at work. And that is cause for hope!

On this day, you are claiming faith in Jesus Christ for yourselves. What begins in baptism is not only being fulfilled at this moment, but continues onward. Hear these words:

_____ [name of confirmand(s)], you are like tree(s) with strong roots drinking in the grace of Jesus Christ.

PEOPLE: **For the realm of God is within you.**

LEADER: _____, you are the illumination that lights up a room, bringing joy to all those around you.

PEOPLE: **For the realm of God is within you.**

LEADER: _____, you are that five hundred-piece puzzle representing the marvelously unique person God made you to be.

PEOPLE: **For the realm of God is within you.**

LEADER: _____, you are like a Tweet, short and to the point, carrying a message of God's hope to the entire world in a way that people will listen.

PEOPLE: **For the realm of God is within you.**

LEADER: _____, you are that five-course meal that nourishes others, feeding both body and the soul.

PEOPLE: For the realm of God is within you.

LEADER: _____, you are that hammer, shattering injustice and building a world where all people are valued.

PEOPLE: For the realm of God is within you.

LEADER: _____, you are that Tesla automobile, bringing innovative answers to the world's biggest challenges.

PEOPLE: For the realm of God is within you.

LEADER: _____, you are that burning candle, bringing light into darkness, as Christ brought light into our world.

ALL: And because the realm of God is within uniquely made and wonderful you, go with our blessing. We pray that through your words, your actions, and the choices you make, God's realm of justice and hope will be fittingly and marvelously made known—to a world desperately in need of it. We ask this in Christ's name. Amen

SUMMONED FOR THE KINGDOM'S STORY

A Confirmation Hymn
1 Thessalonians 2:7, 11–12
Lauda Anima 8.7.8.7.8.7

Summoned for the kingdom's story
God's delight and chosen best.
By this joyful declaration
you affirm God's blessedness.

(Refrain:) Come rejoicing. Come rejoicing,
Praising Christ, for whom we sing.

By the church's exhortation
you were nurtured as one blessed.
May the Spirit hold you steady
in these days and years ahead.

(Refrain)

Justice reigns in fullest measure
when God's kingdom is made known,
knowing in you God has crafted
one whose life Christ's glory shown.

(Refrain)

Other tunes: "Sicilian Mariners" and "Regent Square"

➤ ● ◄

QUESTIONS FOR REFLECTION/ACTION

1. Can you name encounters or lessons learned during your childhood that helped you associate following Christ with the importance of advocacy, constancy, and hope for the future?

2. What specific ways can we better safeguard and nurture the playfulness of children? How might we encourage this quality of liveliness within ourselves?

3. When we baptize a person, the church promises to nurture their faith, claiming them as a beloved child of God. What two things does your faith community do to help make this possible?

➤ ● ◄

After serving in parish ministry for seventeen years, **Gayle A. Murphy** is starting a non-traditional church for those searching for God but alienated by organized religion. Gayle lives in Concord, New Hampshire, where she and her husband are enjoying the empty nest almost as much as they love being an active family with three sons and two grandsons.

Jessica McArdle is a UCC minister and educator, whose interests include research, writing, music, and photography. Having researched the cultivation of lifelong learning and resilience for ministerial leaders, her focus has shifted to developing narratives for whole communities and individuals. A mother of grown children, Jessica and her husband live in the Boston area.

LIFTING THE BURDEN
SEEKING SELF-WORTH IN A CULTURE OF SHAME

51

Shame is the state of believing that one is bad and does not deserve to be loved or to belong. While guilt is understanding that one has done something bad, shame is the understanding that one is bad. Guilt sometimes prefaces a means to return to community by penance or restitution; shame is integral, almost impossible to remove.

Shame isolates us as we come to believe that we are unworthy; when we feel shame, many of us resist connection and withdraw. The church has often been active in "shaming" people. Throughout history, some churches have placed shame at the core of their message—from socially driven exclusionary actions that condemn those they name as outsiders or different, to theologically rooted assertions about specific or general human unworthiness to receive God's love. Shame is not what gathers us together and to God; shame repels, condemns, uproots, and isolates. It is Love that gathers and connects us, that lifts the burden of shame.

PERSONAL PRAYER

We notice shame—and the effects of shame—as we move through our days. It isolates us as we convince ourselves that we are the only ones who have felt this way. Here are two contemplative prayer practices to help break through that boundary.

The Healing Words

Choose a phrase (from scripture, from poetry, etc.) that reminds you of God's love: "I am made in the image of God," "I am God's beloved child; God is well-pleased with me," "You have called me by name, I am yours," "Nothing can separate me from God's love." When you notice feelings of shame creeping in, repeat this phrase in your mind. You might want to incorporate it into your day by "tying" it to something you do daily— for example, praying the phrase five times whenever you drink water, or meditating on it while you walk the dog. Consider writing it down, painting it, hanging it above your bathroom mirror, for instance, so that you see it more and more.

Companions of the Heart

Notice how you are feeling. Are you feeling lonely, depressed, rested, scared, tired, joyful, impatient? As you become aware of how you are feeling, remind yourself that other people—all over the world, from the distant past to today—have felt "just like me." Try to imagine two other people who may have felt just like you do at this moment; imagine how they feel, what they have done, who they are. Imagine that they are sitting or walking beside you, one on either side. Rest in the knowledge that you are not walking alone, and that others are with you. (This is an adaptation and reframing of a Buddhist meditation practice).

COMMUNITY PRAYER

As one way to embody and practice lifting the burden of shame as a community of faith, we can respond to the prayer's repeated remembrance of God's gathering love by moving toward one another. As the bolded text in the prayer is spoken, the individual members of the congregation move together, toward a tangible symbol of God's love—a bowl of water, a flower, a cross, bread and cup. Moving together is a meaningful and healing way to begin naming and dismantling shame. However, touch and nearness hold extraordinary power and can elicit further shame or fear. Be aware of the personal space participants may want as you choose a location for this prayer. Ensure there is plenty of room for all to choose nearness or distance for themselves as they move.

Our God, you have searched us and known us, created and loved us.
You made us for worship, for song and for dance.
You made us for each other, to be gathered together.
In fear, we abandon our dancing and embracing.
We hide away in shame.

Our God, in your love, gather us back.

When shame grips our spirits and whispers our faith is lacking,

Our God, in your love, gather us back.

When shame leaves us frozen in deep isolation,

Our God, in your love, gather us back.

When shame condemns us to solitary suffering,

Our God, in your love, gather us back.

When shame rages, constricting intimacy and compassion,

Our God, in your love, gather us back.

You gather us here to this table,
to this body of wholeness and witness,
to this place of abundance and love.
Amen

→ ▪ ←

QUESTIONS FOR REFLECTION/ACTION

1. Where do you experience shame taking root in your life?

2. How do you see the church and communities you are a part of perpetuating shame or freeing from shame? How could you help a community move from a culture of shame to a culture of unconditional love and acceptance? What practices help us in that journey?

→► • ◄←

Lindsay Popper is a multivocational minister passionate about creative worship, sharing food, and creating spaces of belonging and acceptance. She serves a congregation in Dedham, Massachusetts, and is pursuing ordination in the United Church of Christ.

McKenna E. Lewellen is a writer, teacher, and perpetual student (Rhodes College '14, Boston University '17). She splits her time between her Southern roots in Tennessee and Northern adventures in Massachusetts.

During this final week of reflection, we turn from in-depth topical study to focus more intensely on prayer. Writers from around the world contributed to this chapter with powerful reflections about issues that may affect them, their countries, or the wider global community. Each prayer is, in its way, a question. In these intimate conversations with God, we may not find all of the answers we need, but we can hope that they provide, in equal parts, comfort, challenge, and insight.

⤛ • ⤜

SIMPLEST BEAUTY

by Carolyn Venema

Consider how the wild flowers grow. They do not labor or spin. Yet I tell you, not even Solomon in all his splendor was dressed like one of these. (Luke 12:27)

. . . to stand in awe, immersed in creation—
the softest breeze and warmest sun,
the smallest beetle and buttercups—

humbled, present,
in simple acceptance
of the beauty you created,
made to reflect your own
dense layers of loveliness.

You uncover your face,
like this,
simply to show us
—to tell us—
to help us understand,
with your eyes,
and your heart,
the depth of your own
beauty
craftsmanship
care
all-encompassing love
for us, for all things, lovingly crafted.

Is it your hope that through you
we will also see our own loveliness,
a reflection of the divine within?

For this gift of simple beauty,
we give such profound
and simple thanks.

We are always standing on holy ground.

⤝ • ⤛

Carolyn Venema works in the Ministry of Education in Toronto, Ontario. She's an educator and lifelong learner at heart, and parent to two grown children with whom she has shared many moments of laughter and prayer. She delights in being outdoors, and in gardening in particular.

→» • ‹←

JUSTIÇA AMBIENTAL

by Luiz Carlos Ramos (translation by Paulo Gustavo França)

Ó Deus Eterno,
Ensina-nos a com(+)viver com a natureza:

A amar sua beleza,
A respeitar sua força,
Aresistir à sua fúria.

Ajuda-nos A proteger os seus brotos
A desfrutar de suas sombras,
A partilhar os seus frutos.

Envia teu Espírito e renova a face da terra!
Envia teu Espírito e renova a face da fé!
Envia teu Espírito e renova a face da esperança!
Envia teu Espírito e renova a face da do amor!
Envia teu Espírito e renova a face da vida!

ENVIRONMENTAL JUSTICE

O Eternal God,
Teach us how to live with nature:

To love its beauty,
To respect its power,
To resist its fury.

Help us to protect its buds [*or sprouts*]
To enjoy its shade,
To share its fruits.

Send your Spirit and renew the face of the Earth!
Send your Spirit and renew the face of faith!
Send your Spirit and renew the face of hope!
Send your Spirit and renew the face of love!
Send your Spirit and renew the face of life!

⤝ • ⤙

Luiz Carlos Ramos is a Methodist pastor in Brazil, and also teaches liturgy and homiletics.

⤝ • ⤙

REPRISE

by Laura Martin

Perhaps what Jesus really said was
"I am the bread of life.
whoever comes to me will share my hunger for what can be,"
for what Has Been Started,
for what is born in fragile places.
for the unscripted love in the day's theater,
for what is told in trees that give shade
and birds that lean into the fold of wind.

Whoever looks for me will discover my hunger
for children to learn the cadence of play
rather than the posture of war.
Whoever seeks me will know my
thirst for the long drink of Justice,
found only if we go to wells together,
and for the way we can laugh and pray
and break rules
all the way there.

→▸ • ◂←

Laura Martin is an authorized minister in the United Church of Christ. She worked in homeless services for thirteen years and met many women, men, and children who had experienced insecurity, abuse, war, and lack of sanctuary. She's been deeply impacted by their testimonies in words and in their lives.

→▸ • ◂←

LET ME LIVE

by Eyingbeni Hümtsoe

In my home country of India, a pregnancy can be ended merely because of gender. Every year five hundred thousand fetuses are aborted because they are female (not to speak of the terrible sadness of ten million girls who have been killed after birth in the last twenty years). Prenatal sex determination, although illegal, continues to be conducted.

Let me live; let me not die—
Just because I'm a girl.

I'm conceived out of marriage,
I'll have a birth defect,
I'll be poor,
I'll be parentless,
I'll have many siblings,

Let me live; let me not die—
Just because—
My father won't acknowledge me,
My mother doesn't want me,
Family will not have me,
Community would mock my birth,
Church would mark my origin.

Let me live; let me not die—
I want to soar heights,
Dive depths,
Wander across the world,
Live my dreams,
Marry and have children,
Build a home, a nation, a Church.

I want to live; I don't want to die.
Let me live; let me not die.

Let me live; let me not die—
Because—
God has formed me,
Knows how I came to be,
Sees what I can be,
Beholds me with compassion,
Justifies me with grace.

⊰ • ⊱

Eyingbeni Hümtsoe is a proud tribal who teaches Christian doctrines and gender theologies. He's a silent peace practitioner and a loud proponent of truth, justice, and equality. He loves his daughter, Enya Tsalü, and sees all girls with the same eyes as he sees her. He believes that women are the most exquisite design of God and that if there's any hope of mending the broken pieces in the world, women should lead the way.

⊰ • ⊱

TO TEST OR TO EDUCATE: THAT IS THE QUESTION

by Elaine S. Gaetani

Gracious God, am I good enough? Will I cut muster, make the grade, pass the test, show my worth? If I flunk this test, which makes me so nervous and squirm in my seat, will I still be able to stay with my friends in my class? Will I be labeled, left out, left behind? What will my parents say? Will you still love me?

I am confused, my God and my Friend, because I have come to know You as a God of creativity, spontaneity, curiosity, experimentation, and faith in all the different kinds of cleverness in the human spirit.

Is there a standardized test for that? Will they ever know my true gifts and talents?

God, be with me now, as I sharpen my pencil, gulp down the lump in my throat, and calm the knot in my belly. Help me to remember to never stop learning even though I hate the testing. Show me again and again, Brilliant God, that Love can't be measured, creativity can't be harnessed, and the human spirit is far too great to test with any human educational standards.

Let them not break my spirit, Your spirit in me.
Amen

→ • ←

Life-long learner, teacher, pastoral counselor/spiritual director, and ordained minister, **Elaine S. Gaetani** has long been called to help co-create a more just, loving, safe, and hopeful environment for children of all ages. It is her experience that this starts with faith, love, and God's grace.

→ • ←

THE MITTEN TREE

by Arlene L. Drennan

Every fall when Jack Frost chases
the warmth of late summer to the next year
a child-size tree springs
from the hardening ground.

Growing children wander near
the Mitten Tree
in search of warmth and shelter
from their whirling world.

One child looks for satisfaction
from her growling tummy.
Too little food, every day, and
no family time at a kitchen table

She passes the Mitten Tree—
a mitten falls into her hands

One child seeks protection
from outside enemies,
the bullies and the standardized tests
trying to fit his body into
a hard hiding place.

He passes the Mitten Tree—
a mitten falls into his hands

One child cries for a toy
that will be her own,
Or a pet that she can care for
that no one will remove from her life

She passes the Mitten Tree—
a mitten falls into her hands

One child sits in silence and
waits for someone who will listen
someone who wants to hear his dream
and who will smile with him

He passes the Mitten Tree—
a mitten falls into his hands

These mittens of food,
safe spaces, a treasure to hold,
listeners, and dreams—
still, someone must be knitting.

Who will tend the Mitten Tree?

⇥ • ⇤

Arlene L. Drennan is a native Iowan, raised in the rich heartland of farming. Her church life has its core in a small rural church. She is a commissioned minister for the Church of Christ—Disciples of Christ in the Upper Midwest. She's never known hunger or abuse.

⇥ • ⇤

A PRAYER FOR YOUNG CHILDREN WHO MUST TAKE CARE OF PARENTS

by Cathy Hasty

Loving Abba,
I am a motherless or fatherless child. I do not get the attentive care that I see others have at my age. Instead I have to be the caregiver to my care-givers. I feel disappointed, confused, and alone. Sometimes I wonder if I am damaged. Sometimes I feel I am superhuman. These are both ways I have managed this overwhelming challenge.

Powerful God, I call upon you to come to me as the source of wisdom and of care. I need to remember that every moment you are wooing me towards a future more loving than my present. You are giving me assurance that I am safe. I will be safe. I need to remember that you do not ever shame or condemn me for my fears or my insecurity or the crazy ways I try to get my needs met. You invite me to know that I can be both strong and weak, both wise and foolish, both independent and dependent. You reassure me that I am not the problem.

You know, Abba, that there have been times when I was expected to know more, do more, be more than I could as a child or young person. I have been expected to deal with chaos or be the fully functioning adult rather than the one who is nurtured, directed, given care. In the name of truth, I need to proclaim that the structures on which I sought to depend have not been reliable. They ask me to listen to them, instead of listening to me. They expect me to take care of them instead of caring for me. They want me to set boundaries on them instead of setting limits on me.

I need to cry out that I have been abandoned, overlooked, used in ways that hurt me. I cry out that I have been scared, knowing that the adults on whom I rely are unstable and even hurtful. In the face of this abandonment and this abuse, I have pulled myself into shapes and put myself into spaces that I cannot sustain. I have forced myself to perform in ways that are inhuman and inhumane to myself and sometimes to others. I have paid a price for these demands. At times I wonder if I am broken or inadequate. I feel lost. I have done too much or too little, acted nicer than I feel or meaner than I want to be. Now I know that in these and other ways, I tried to protect myself and others.

In this moment, I call upon your strength, your mercy, and your love as I admit that I, in my fear, have hurt myself and others. I have been tired and I have given up. I have been wired and out of control. These have been my responses to the overwhelming demands and the profound confusion. I have struggled to know who I am as I negotiate a complex world without the gradual and loving nurture from those more mature.

With this prayer, I rest in the assurance that change is occurring at a level out of my awareness. I call upon the holy forces that are seeking to give me solace. I open myself to healing and to love. You are there offering love beyond my imagination. I am seeking to remain open to the possibilities. I will look for ways to be kind and to receive kindness. I will seek to speak the truth in love when it is safe and will make some difference. I will find places to be vulnerable when it is safe. I will be wise as a serpent and gentle as a dove by seeking out the forces of good in the world, knowing that you are seeking me out and will never, ever give up on me.

In the name of all that is holy, all that is loving, and all that is sacred, I pray. Amen

⤜ ● ⤛

Cathy Hasty writes and paints out of a quirky sense of faithfulness. More about her and her work can be found at www.cathyhasty.com. She would love to hear from you.

⤜ ● ⤛

ORAÇÃO PELOS JOVENS

by Luiz Carlos Ramos (translation by Paulo Gustavo França)

Senhor, agradecemos-te
pelos jovens que temos e pelos jovens que fomos;
pela juventude que vemos e pela juventude que tivemos;
pelos jovens que estão entre nós e pelo jovem que ainda está dentro de cada um de nós.

Agradecemos-te
pela transformação permanente do mundo que os jovens promovem
e pela transformação constante que tu fazes na vida de cada jovem.

Senhor, tu que fazes novas todas as coisas,
não permitas que estes jovens se conformem com o presente século;
que não sejam formados pela mídia, pela moda ou pelos maus modos;
que sejam antes transformados pela renovação da mente
e pela oferta dos seus corpos como sacrifício vivo, santo e agradável a ti.

Que estes jovens não sejam meramente alegres, mas felizes;
que não sejam somente saudáveis, mas conscientes;
que não sejam apenas fortes, mas tolerantes;
que não cresçam unicamente em estatura, mas em graça;
que não sejam só inteligentes, mas que se tornem sábios;
que não sejam crédulos, mas crentes;
que não sejam jovens na aparência, mas na essência;
enfim, que não sejam fruto do presente século,
mas filhos e filhas do Deus vivo
    para que vivam o Amor,
    que promovam a Paz,
    e pratiquem a Justiça.
Oramos
em nome de Jesus Cristo,
o jovem que não somente revolucionou o mundo com suas ideias,
mas salvou a humanidade com seu amor.
Amém

→> • <←

PRAYER FOR YOUNG PEOPLE

God, we thank you
for the young people we have now and for the young people we once were;
for the youth we see now and for the youth we once had;
for the young men and women in our midst and for the young man and
    woman that still lives within each of us.

We thank you
for the ongoing transformation of the world the youth foster
and for the constant transformation you cause in the life of each youth.

God who makes all things new,
keep these young people from conforming to this present age;
that they may not be formed by the media, by today's trends
    or bad habits;
but that they may be transformed by the renewing of the mind
and by the gift of their bodies as a living offering, holy and
    pleasing to you.

That these young men and women may not be merely happy, but joyful;
that they may not be only healthy, but mindful;
that they may not be just strong, but open-minded;
that they may not be only intelligent, but that they may become wise;
that they may not be youthful in their look, but in their essence;
in a word, that they may not be the child of this present culture,
but sons and daughters of the Living God,
    so they may embody the Love,
    work for Peace,
    and may practice Justice.
We pray
in the name of Jesus Christ,
the young person who not only revolutionized the world with his ideas,
but also saved humankind with his love.
Amen

→- • -←-

Luiz Carlos Ramos is a Methodist pastor in Brazil, and also teaches liturgy and homiletics.

→- • -←-

GOD'S LOVE OF ALL, REGARDLESS OF SEXUAL ORIENTATION

by Gerardo C. C. Oberman (translation by Kati Baruja)

"Tú me formaste en el vientre de mi madre . . ." (Salmo 139:13)

Me han dicho muchas veces
que soy una obra imperfecta, que soy anormal,
que me he desviado, que vivo en perversión,
que soy una abominación a tus ojos,
mi Dios creador.

Me han lastimado con esas frases
y muchas más que no me atrevo a contarte.
Me han herido con insultos, desprecios,
maltratos, golpes, negaciones, vejaciones . . .
Una, diez, cien veces me han matado.
Y en cada ocasión, miles aplaudían
y otros miles callaban,
incluso quienes se dicen tus hijos e hijas.

Me han odiado y me odian
por tratar de vivir libre, honesta y abiertamente
mi sexualidad.
En tu nombre me han condenado,
en tu nombre me han expulsado,

en tu nombre me han discriminado.
Y en tu nombre han cometido
toda clase de atrocidades
con quienes no queremos
que nos encierren en ningún closet.

Pero yo sé, materno Dios,
que tú me formaste
en el vientre de quien me dio la vida.
Maravillosamente me hiciste
y en tu corazón me pensaste gay.
A tu imagen y semejanza me hiciste:
lesbiana, gay, homosexual.

No hay ningún pecado
en vivir conforme a tu designio amoroso,
de acuerdo a tu perfecta obra en mí.
Quienes me odian y me condenan,
te odian y te condenan a ti;
quienes me lastiman y me matan,
te lastiman y te matan a ti;
quienes me miran y se burlan y me insultan,
se burlan de ti y te insultan a ti.

Yo te doy gracias, Dios de lo diverso,
porque me pensaste y me hiciste
tal como soy, a tu propia imagen.
"Te alabo porque estoy maravillado,
porque es maravilloso lo que has hecho.
¡De ello estoy bien convencido!" (Salmo 139:14)

"You formed me in my mother's womb . . . ." (Psalm 139:13)

I've been told many times
that I'm an imperfect creation, that I'm not normal,
that I've turned away from the good path, that I live in perversion,

that I'm an abomination in your eyes,
O God my creator.

I have been hurt by those words
and many others that I don't dare to tell you.
They have hurt me with insults, put-downs,
mistreatment, punches, denials, humiliations . . .
Once, ten times, a hundred times they've killed me.
And every time, thousands applaud
and thousands more remain silent,
even those that call themselves your children.

They have hated me and they hate me
for trying to live my sexuality
freely, honestly and openly.
In your name they have condemned me,
in your name they have expelled me,
in your name they have discriminated against me.
And in your name they have committed
all kinds of atrocities
against those of us who don't want them
to enclose us in any closet.

But I know, maternal God,
that you formed me
in the womb of the one who gave me life.
You made me marvelously
and in your heart you dreamed me up gay.
You made me in your image:
lesbian, gay, homosexual.

There is no sin
in living according to your loving design,
according to your perfect work in me.
Those who hate me and condemn me
hate you and condemn you;

those who hurt me and kill me
hurt you and kill you;
those who see me and mock me and insult me,
mock you and insult you.

I give you thanks, O God of the diverse,
because you thought me up and you made me
just as I am, in your own image.
"I praise you, for I am fearfully and wonderfully made.
Wonderful are your works;
that I know very well!" (Psalm 139:14)

→► • ◄←

Gerardo C. C. Oberman is a songwriter, poet, and pastor in the Reformed Churches in Argentina and current president of the denomination. In 2004 he cofounded Red Crearte, a Latin American liturgical network, and continues to coordinate the work. He also serves as historian of the Reformed churches in Argentina and the Dutch immigration in the region.

→► • ◄←

ON BENDED KNEE

by Maria Mankin

God, I've always shied away from teams, from labeling myself
with a number or a brightly colored jersey, on the field or in the stands.
You know I hid from Friday night lights, from the face painting and
        friendly rivalries
of high school football, how "sick" I was the day of tennis tryouts—

sick of having to pretend I cared at all about the cheering and camaraderie
of sweat-bound sisters and brothers.

You know me, God. You know I've cherished a few stolen moments
    of athleticism—
grindingly slow and solitary runs, inflexible yogic moments of peace—
all on my own, all in service to my own body, my own spirit.
No one to high five but my own reflection, no one to cheer me on
but a whispered prayer that pushed me a bit further.

And yet, God, I find myself wanting to take a knee.
I ache to stand among my black brothers on the field,
to lend a little of the privilege of this skin to their cause,
aware it costs me nothing. History will paint people
like me heroes without question, sheltering us from spit and rage
and the crippling danger of being born with dark skin,
while my struggling brothers risk everything to be heard and seen
without prejudice. They will kneel in the dirt and endure
the consequences of their bravery, as they have for hundreds of years.

I may not fit on a team, God, I may not know that holy solidarity,
but I can't imagine standing while one of my sisters knelt in the dirt—
not after days or months or years of working and celebrating beside her.
The chance to kneel, to pray, to beseech others to examine
    their privilege
seems like such a small gesture of love—the right to such protest
    a divine gift,
a hail Mary for a country that has been bent under by the victors of hate.

God, I ask that you kneel within each of us who stands by as these
    men risk
their livelihoods and their lives to bear silent, gracious witness to the truth.
I ask for a place on their team, a sign I might raise in solidarity,
    a cheer for equality
that I may hold in my heart and sing forth in honor of their fearless
    faith and play for justice.

I ask this in the name of your redeeming spirit, which is never blind to
  small signs of change
or deaf to voices that speak hope and power in places we don't expect
  them.
Amen

→→ • ←←

Maria Mankin has published five resource books with Pilgrim Press, as well as contributed to several poetry and essay anthologies. She writes a weekly literary review,
Books J'adore (booksjadore.com), with an audience of twenty-five thousand, and
recently published *Circ*, a collaborative novel with Pigeon Park Press. She is currently
working on a second novel as well as a children's book.

→→ • ←←

PSALM OF RESURRECTION FOR A SON IN PRISON

by Barbara Wass VanAusdall

How amazing!
The darkness of Good Friday has left my soul
and in its place is the sunrise of Easter.
I am a new person,
  still mother
child
  sister
    wife
      friend,
but the adjectives have changed.
    Gone are despairing, rejected, empty, hopeless, depressed . . .

Instead, I am hopeful,
> I am at peace,
>> I am joyful
>>> I am LOVE

God is tangible in my daily walk
God is in every visit with my son.

And my son is brand new, freed from his grave, learning to live with his mistakes, knowing he is held in God's arms.

In you, O God, he is whole, asking for your help to live one day at a time, giving you control over all he is and will become.
Amen

→➤ • ◄←

Barbara Wass VanAusdall's career teaching second language speakers who came to the states escaping injustice, discrimination, and abuse, as well as local students caught in difficult situations, sensitized her to injustices that could not be ignored. She addressed them in class projects and in shared conversations and activities with students. She continues to do so as a retiree through her music and writings, work as a lay minister, and issues in her own family.

→➤ • ◄←

AFTER DISASTER ... (originally, CHRISTCHURCH AFTER THE EARTHQUAKE)

by Beverley L. Osborn

This broken city
looks nothing like my childhood memories
of pigeons wheeling over tall buildings,
of the fine architecture
lovingly created by our forebears,
the trees they planted that grew to statuesque majesty,
the beautiful, beloved city I was proud to call home.
I mourned that when my children grew up
their memories would be of rubble and dust and loss
and weeds growing in desolate open spaces.

But I was wrong!
My children will remember not buildings, but community—
the strong and loving support of strangers who became family,
the fun activities, the welling up of joy and healing and purpose,
a way of life built on sharing and generosity and relationships
that will be their strong foundation forever.

Long ago, on the Mount of Transfiguration,
Peter and James and John saw the glory of God in Jesus.
Their immediate desire was to safely house and contain that glory.
But Jesus smiled and led them down the mountain
to build love and healing and hope and kindness in people.

I need not fear.
My children will have a heritage of memories
even more valuable than mine.

(Thanks to Sara Templeton, whose news article on the earthquake inspired me.)

→> ● <←

Beverley L. Osborn is officially retired from Methodist ministry in New Zealand, but is occupied in local church, having added morning tea, church flowers, manse cleaning, and meeting and greeting rosters to worship and fill-in preaching. Spare time? Gardening, knitting for all local new babies and toddlers, trying to retrain tuis (bush birds) to sing cadences instead of newly acquired wolf whistles.

⤙ • ⤚

A PRAYER FOR EQUAL PAY

by Michelle L. Torigian

Mother God, carrier of all hope, we bear layers of discouragement as we walk with you. Our dignity has been diluted by what others believe we deserve.

The frustration builds within us as we work. *Why have we accepted less for so long? Why are laws not protecting us? Why do our fellow people of faith vote against legislation that will protect us? Do they not understand that our work is equally valuable? Do they not realize that we have families to support as well?*

When we look at the statistics, we see that vocations in which females dominate receive less compensation. *Mother God, how can some occupations—especially ones of service, like teaching, nursing and social work—be deemed less valuable?*

As women take time off for families, we lose tenure in our occupations, impacting what we may earn when returning to the workforce. And in some professions, women are encouraged less to apply for advanced positions. All of these discrepancies impact not only our current pay but also our future incomes, as retirement savings are much lower for those of us who make less money.

Yet, when we think of the gender pay gap, some of us must remember that we hold more privilege. While our white brothers make a considerable amount more than most of us, our sisters of color bear the burden of making less because of their race or ethnicity. As we work for equality, may we always remember that all of us deserve to make as much as the most privileged in our society, and let us not leave any of our sisters behind.

Give us the courage to ask for more: equal pay and salaries that dignify our talents and knowledge. Help us to still find the light within ourselves as we advocate and wait for fair treatment. We are made in your image no matter how we are compensated or recognized. Amen

→≻ ● ≺←

Michelle L. Torigian is the pastor of St. Paul United Church of Christ, Old Blue Rock, in Cincinnati, Ohio. A 2010 graduate of Eden Theological Seminary, Torigian has had essays in the books *There's a Woman in the Pulpit* (Skylight Paths Publishing) and *Sacred Habits: The Rise of the Creative Clergy* (Noesis Press). Her writings can be found at the Huffington Post Religion page, RevGalBlogPals, the UCC's New Sacred, and her own blog, michelletorigian.com.

→≻ ● ≺←

MONEY IN POLITICS

by Richard Bott

When another Pharisee
(or lobbyist, or corporation, or country)
pours hundreds,
or thousands,
or thousands more
(Euro or Lira, Peso or Pound,
and especially the "Almighty Dollar")
into the coffers of the ones who

make the decisions,
I wonder, God.
I wonder about "back scratching,"
about "breach of trust,"
about whose livelihood,
and whose lives,
really matter.

But then I remember the Widow's gift.
Not just the coin,
but what it represented:
not only her resources,
but all of her, herself.

And then I remember
there are a lot more Widows,
and children,
and real, everyday people,
than there are lobbies
or interest groups,
or campaign contributions,
or bribes
that can be made.

Help me to remember that,
God of hope.
Help our leaders to remember that,
God of justice.
Help us all act on that,
God of love.

Let it be so.

⊱ ● ⊰

A pastor, poet, and liturgical writer, **Richard Bott** serves in ministry with the United Church of Canada in Vancouver, British Columbia. He celebrates that people find his words helpful in their ministries.

→➤ • ◄←

A PRAYER FOR VOTING RIGHTS

by Michelle L. Torigian

God of balance and Driver of justice, we are called to voice our conscience. We are asked by you to uphold justice and kindness. Voting is one of the ways we are called to be this influence in our world.

We thought an amendment to our constitution would allow for people of color to vote. But some found ways to limit rights. We thought that the successful suffrage movement allowed all women to vote, but sisters of color were starved of opportunities as well. Even after additional voting rights acts were signed into law, some in our society still hunt for ways to skirt justice.

Many of us are ready to bring the blazing fire of your Spirit into our world through a vote, and yet we must walk away without marking a ballot.

The long lines at the polls force some to reconsider what time they can afford to spend in accomplishing this task. The polling places are too far away, and transportation is inadequate. Work schedules reduce the time available to travel to the polls. Affordable child care is scarce. Money for a babysitter is not available.

Some of our neighbors have a tough time attaining an ID document. They no longer drive, and the need for identification is minimal. Others have little money to fund the credentials.

And then there our sisters and brothers who just want to vote again. Living in states that refuse to restore their voting rights after incarceration makes this privilege an unattainable dream. Sentences have been completed, but our government still does not afford them the rights of their citizenship.

When electoral college results give us a different president-elect than the popular vote winner, we wonder if our system is beyond broken. Our hearts sink low, leading us into greater despair. We turn to you in our confusion and set our devastation before you.

Our frustration grows as we think of all of the ways those in power obstruct their neighbors' rights to vote. From mass incarceration to poverty, from time constraints to distance, many insincere rules beg us to think that our vote doesn't matter. As we await the next election, and the next election and the next, God, open roads, wallets, and minds to extend rights to all of us—from the suburbs to urban areas to small towns. Amen

→→ ● ←←

Michelle L. Torigian is the pastor of St. Paul United Church of Christ, Old Blue Rock, in Cincinnati, Ohio. A 2010 graduate of Eden Theological Seminary, Torigian has had essays in the books *There's a Woman in the Pulpit* (Skylight Paths Publishing) and *Sacred Habits: The Rise of the Creative Clergy* (Noesis Press). Her writings can be found at the Huffington Post Religion page, RevGalBlogPals, the UCC's New Sacred, and her own blog, michelletorigian.com.

→→ ● ←←

PRAYER FOR REFUGEES, A PRAYER FROM GERMANY

by Detlev Knoche

Guter Gott,
Wir danken Dir für unsere weltweiten ökumenischen Beziehungen
    und für unsere Schwestern und Brüder in allen Teilen dieser Welt.
Du willst uns ein Leben in Fülle schenken,
aber dies Leben wird immer wieder verletzt und eingeschränkt:
da wo Gewalt, Terror, und Krieg herrschen,
da wo sich Menschen mit Waffen bekämpfen—
mit Waffen die auch in unserem Land produziert werden.
Guter Gott,
Wir bitten für alle Opfer von Kriegen und Bürgerkriegen;
Wir bitten Dich um Deine Kraft für alle, die sich gegen die
    Waffenexporte einsetzen
und für Frieden, Gerechtigkeit, und die Bewahrung der Schöpfung
    eintreten.
Guter Gott,
Dein eigener Sohn Jesus Christus war ein Flüchtling.
Wir bitten für alle Menschen die vor Kriegen, Unterdrückung,
    oder vor Armut fliehen. Sei ihnen nahe!
Guter Gott,
wir beten für unsere Regierung dass sie unsere Grenzen öffnen für all
    die Menschen die einen sicheren Platz und Hilfe suchen.
Amen!

Gracious God,
We are thankful for worldwide ecumenical fellowship
    and for our sisters and brothers all around the world.
God, you want to grant us a life in fullness, but it is restricted
where violence, terror, and war rule,
where human beings fight against each other with weapons—
with weapons also produced in our own country.
Gracious God,
we pray for all the victims of wars and civil wars;

we ask you to strengthen us in the struggles against arms exports
and to stand for peace, justice, and the integrity of creation.
Gracious God,
your Son Jesus Christ himself was a refugee. We pray for all those who
    flee from war, persecution or out of poverty. Be close to them.
God, we pray for our government that they may open our borders to
    those who need safe refuge and help.
Amen!

→▸ • ◂←

Detlev Knoche was born in 1958 and is pastor of the Protestant Church in Hesse and
Nassau (EKHN), director of the Ecumenical Center of EKHN and of the Evangelical
Church of Kurhessen-Waldeck, and Ecumenical Liaison Officer of EKHN.

→▸ • ◂←

A PRAYER OF CONFESSION FOR MY PART IN TERRORISM

by R. Matthew Stevens (author's translations from the Anishinaabemowin)

G'zhem-mnidoo *(Creator of All Things):*
It is hard to love the balaclava shrouded brother with a Kalashnikov
    in his hand.
I don't know how to get close to the sister with a suicide vest
    under her burqa.
Yet I know that the profit motive of a weapons-maker on the other side
    of my town provided the bullets for that gun,
And that the calculated indifference of some local Internet service
    promptly circulated the plans for those explosives.
While my self-indulgence, safely ensconced within the bastion of our
    sham Christianity, reduced brothers and sisters to terrorists.

Gizhe-manidoowiwin *(Spirit of Divine Nature):*
I know I abrogated compassion, and through fear empowered a militaristic response from our evolving quasi-police state.
I gave tacit approval to the security merchants to squander more wealth than would feed all the world's hungry.
I've remained silent as some politician restricted yet another human right in the name of antiterrorism.
I convinced myself there's nothing to do about my country putting boots on the ground in a sister's and brother's homeland.
Or to relieve the resulting devastation and social chaos when they brought our troops back as homeless and wounded veterans.

Manidoowag *(Spirit of Connectedness):*
It is you who speaks to us of our connectedness, and that nothing occurs in isolation.
It is clear that I need to relearn your wise teaching, and abandon the foolish notion of self-sufficiency.
I sincerely grieve for the harm my self-indulgence has unwittingly done to those I have never even met.
For those whom we've reduced to believing they've nothing left to lose, help me share with them a true measure of their value.
And may I be as determined a healer of terrorism as I have been as an instigator of terrorism in others.
Chii-Miigwech *(profound thanks)* Amen

→▸ • ◂←

R. Matthew Stevens: Being a person of Métis heritage (sometime referred to as "mixed blood") I consider myself particularly fortunate to be able to occupy a space between cultures, with access to both. I've been privileged to learn many of the traditional teachings from some very gifted and patient Elders, and to have availed myself of some excellent formal education as well. From both of these sources I have learned how disabling a pervasive sense of guilt can be to an individual, and how collectively it can incapacitate society from appropriately redressing prevailing circumstances.

➤➤ • ◄◄

SÚPLICAS E INTERCESSÕES

by Luiz Carlos Ramos (translation by Paulo Gustavo França)

Deus Vivo e Eterno,
Lembramo-nos, nesta hora, de toda a família humana,
especialmente aquelas famílias que têm fome de comida
    e sede de justiça,
daquelas que perderam suas casas e sua dignidade.

[Silêncio]

Lembramo-nos dos que choram sobre seus mortos
e temem por suas vidas.

[Silêncio]

Lembramo-nos da tua Igreja,
estabelecida neste e em outroslugares,
para acender e disseminar a luz da tua graça e da tua verdade.

[Silêncio]

Lembramo-nos daqueles e daquelas que estão doentes,
    que estão sofrendo,
que têm decisões difíceis a tomar,
especialmente aqueles e aquelas que nos pediram para que
    intercedêssemos em seu favor.
Por isso, nesta hora, confiados em tua infinita misericórdia,
apresentamos-te os nomes desses nossos irmãos e irmãs:

[Nomes . . .]

Em silêncio, Senhor, apresentamos diante de ti, ainda,
aqueles nomes que não podemos mencionar em voz alta . . .

[Silêncio]

Por fim, depositamos em tuas mãos, Deus Vivo e Eterno,
nossas tarefas inconclusas, nossos problemas insolúveis,
nossas esperanças não cumpridas, nossas preocupações, angústias,
    e frustrações,
sabendo que somente aquilo que tu abençoas é que haverá
    de prosperar.

[Silêncio]

Esta é a oração que fazemos
em nome de Jesus Cristo, Senhor e Salvador nosso.
Amém

SUPPLICATIONS AND INTERCESSIONS

Living and Eternal God,
We remember, at this hour, the whole human family,
especially those families that are hungry for food and thirsty for justice,
those that have lost their homes and dignity.

[Silence]

We remember those who weep over their dead,
and who are fearful for their lives.

[Silence]

We remember your Church,
established here and in other places,
to light up and make known the light of your grace and truth.

[Silence]

We remember those who are sick, who are suffering,
[who] have difficult decisions to make,
especially the ones who have asked us to lift them up in prayer.
And so, at this hour, leaning on your infinite mercy,
we bring before you the names of our brothers and sisters:

[Names . . .]

In silence, God, we also place before you,
Those names we cannot say aloud . . .

[Silence]

And then, we put in your hands, Living and Eternal God,
our unfinished tasks, our unsolvable problems,
our hopes not attained, our worries, anxieties, and frustrations,
confident that only that which you bless will prosper.

[Silence]

This is the prayer we make
in the name of Jesus Christ, our Lord and Savior.
Amen

→→ • ←←

Luiz Carlos Ramos is a Methodist pastor in Brazil, and also teaches liturgy and homiletics.

→→ • ←←

NOT IN MY IMAGE

Laura Martin

I did not make hands in my image
for them to pull triggers
and carry out instant death sentences
against my beloveds.

I did not make humankind in my image
for them to yell "Crucify, crucify,"
to construct higher walls to
keep each other out.

I did not make children in my image
for them to learn to distract themselves
from their hungers
for food and for belonging.

I did not make you in my image
to believe you are created from anything
but agape love and the wisdom and strength
to bring my image back again.

⤜ ● ⤛

Laura Martin is an authorized minister in the United Church of Christ. She worked in
homeless services for thirteen years and met many women, men, and children who had
experienced insecurity, abuse, war, and lack of sanctuary. She's been deeply impacted
by their testimonies in words and in their lives.

⤜ ● ⤛